Taking Control of Writing Your Thesis

ALSO AVAILABLE FROM BLOOMSBURY

Reflective Teaching in Higher Education, Paul Ashwin
Successful Dissertations, Mark O'Hara, Caron Carter,
    Pam Dewis, Janet Kay and Jonathan Wainwright
What are Qualitative Research Ethics?, Rose Wiles
What is Diary Method?, Ruth Bartlett and Christine Milligan
What is Discourse Analysis?, Stephanie Taylor
What is Inclusive Research?, Melanie Nind
What is Narrative Research?, Corinne Squire,
    Mark Davis, Cigdem Esin, Molly Andrews, Barbara Harrison,
    Lars-Christer Hydén and Margareta Hydén
What is Online Research?, Tristram Hooley,
    Jane Wellens & John Marriott
What is Qualitative Interviewing?, Rosalind Edwards
    and Janet Holland
What is Qualitative Research?, Martyn Hammersley
What is Social Network Analysis?, John Scott

Forthcoming from Bloomsbury:

What are Community Studies?, Graham Crow
What is Qualitative Longitudinal Research?, Bren Neale
What is Quantitative Longitudinal Data Analysis?, Vernon Gayle
    and Paul Lambert
What is Rhythmanalysis?, Dawn Lyon

Taking Control of Writing Your Thesis

A Guide to Get You to the End

KAY GUCCIONE AND JERRY WELLINGTON

Bloomsbury Academic
An imprint of Bloomsbury Publishing Plc

B L O O M S B U R Y
LONDON · OXFORD · NEW YORK · NEW DELHI · SYDNEY

Bloomsbury Academic

An imprint of Bloomsbury Publishing Plc

50 Bedford Square	1385 Broadway
London	New York
WC1B 3DP	NY 10018
UK	USA

www.bloomsbury.com

BLOOMSBURY and the Diana logo are trademarks of Bloomsbury Publishing Plc

First published 2017

British Library Cataloguing-in-Publication Data

A catalogue record for this book is available from the British Library.

ISBN: HB: 978-1-4742-8295-6
PB: 978-1-4742-8294-9
epDF: 978-1-4742-8296-3
ePub: 978-1-4742-8297-0

Library of Congress Cataloging-in-Publication Data

Names: Guccione, Kay, author. | Wellington, J. J. (Jerry J.), author.
Title: Taking control of writing your thesis: a guide to get you to the end / Kay Guccione and Jerry Wellington.
Description: New York: Bloomsbury Academic, An imprint of Bloomsbury Publishing Plc, 2017. | Includes bibliographical references and index.
Identifiers: LCCN 2017004461| ISBN 9781474282956 (hardback) | ISBN 9781474282949 (paperback) | ISBN 9781474282963 (epdf) | ISBN 9781474282970 (epub)
Subjects: LCSH: Dissertations, Academic–Handbooks, manuals, etc. | Dissertations, Academic–United Kingdom–Handbooks, manuals, etc.
Classification: LCC LB2369 .G83 2017 | DDC 378.2–dc23
LC record available at https://lccn.loc.gov/2017004461

Cover image © nico_blue/Getty Images

Typeset by Deanta Global Publishing Services, Chennai, India

CONTENTS

Preface vi

1 Writing as a partnered enterprise 1

2 Writing milestones and crunch points 21

3 The parallel processes of research doing and research writing 37

4 Writing and thinking as partner processes 59

5 Reading and writing as joint functions 79

6 Bringing your writing and the literature together harmoniously 93

7 How to coach yourself through thesis writing 107

8 How to stop writing your thesis 133

9 Finishing your thesis with the *viva* in mind and finding a life thereafter 151

References 167
Index 174

PREFACE

This book was inspired by our experiences of working with stressed or overwhelmed doctoral thesis writers. Kay coaches thesis writers, and has used her research on the barriers to thesis writing to design a Thesis Mentoring programme in which over 350 students have been paired with a postdoc mentor. Jerry has many years' experience of doctoral supervision and examination on PhD and EdD programmes, and has further supported and developed students and supervisors through his former role as a head of research degrees. In effect we have co-created this book with hundreds of thesis writers and thesis mentors, and our role on writing it has been to curate and interpret what we have seen into a format you will find useful.

We do feel that developing authoritative academic writing has distinct advantages if it is a continual process of writing and feedback that starts early and continues throughout the whole degree. However, we do understand that some students enter a 'writing up period' with very little previous writing experience. Splitting the doctorate into 'research doing' and 'research writing' is still very much the predominant mode in many places, in particular in science and engineering disciplines. This book is not an 'ideal guide' to writing your thesis, and it does not assume you have plenty of time to get things in order and build up your writing expertise. Reading it, you won't find lessons on 'what you should have done' or advice that you'd need to go back in time to put into practice. Rather, this is a pragmatic approach that will take you from today up to your thesis submission deadline and will help you make a plan and stay on track. The main message we hope to convey in this book is that it's not too late for you to get started with thesis writing, or to take control of the thesis. We have selected the examples and quotes we use throughout in order to demonstrate to you that your experiences of and reactions to thesis writing are not uncommon, and we hope you are buoyed by the fact that you are not alone.

Through this book we want to share with you a body of ideas, advice and ways of working that we have collected and collated from the students we work with, in effect bringing you insider opinions on thesis writing from other students who are writing. Through our work of supervising, examining, mentoring and coaching doctoral students collectively, we have met hundreds of thesis writers – many who are self-define as having become stuck, stressed or burned out from writing. Each of these students is an individual, with different preferred ways of working. Each has approached thesis writing in their own way and found different parts of the writing either more difficult or easier.

Writing about research can seem hard to get to grips with because you are using different and unfamiliar ways of thinking compared with those you used in the 'doing' of research. It can be easy to fall into the trap of assuming that because you have done the research, the recording of that research should be relatively easy; but writing at the doctoral level isn't about simply describing what you have done. In our opinion you have to get started and trust the process. Try to think about writing as a daily practice for which you gain understanding and enjoyment by writing regularly, not as a skill set you can pick up by reading about it. Thesis writing is a learning process that will take some time and effort to become comfortable with. Focus on the idea that practice, with feedback, makes perfect – or somewhere close enough.

Most students experience emotional highs and lows throughout the doctorate. Some thesis writers, or 'should-be thesis writers', can at times get stuck repeating unhelpful habits, ways of thinking or ways of working with others, which cause them to experience delay, anxiety or paralysis in the writing process. Our specialism is in helping this particular group of writers to understand what's happening to them, change their approach and self-manage the process to regain a sense of command and authority. Here we hope to share our learning in a way that is useful to you too. This book will not be a list of potential thesis pitfalls offered up to frighten you. We don't intend to put obstacles in your way without acknowledging that they can be overcome with some considered thinking and planning.

We do acknowledge though, that feeling stuck or overwhelmed by thesis writing is not always due to the habits and behaviours of you, the student. We know that managing your supervisor, or supervisory team, is not an easy thing to do. In this book we will offer guidance that you can use to help your supervisor to help you. We will demonstrate how you could better manage a conversation with your supervisor, ask for the feedback you need, and coordinate the multiple types of guidance and input you are receiving. We also make suggestions about other sources of support for writing that you can seek out or create for yourself. Our focus is on helping you to achieve open dialogue and communication, which can help you move towards professional partnership that is defined and bounded. We know that different structures exist across different institutions and disciplines, and we will use the term 'supervisor' to mean either a single supervisor or a supervisory team. We understand the challenges that came with managing the input and guidance of multiple supervisors and at times will specifically refer to managing multiple supervisors.

This book has been created to be appropriate for all types of doctoral students in all kinds of research institutions, and we feel that master's degree students may also benefit from the ideas and exercises in this book. We use the word 'thesis' throughout to describe the physical output of a doctoral degree. You may be more familiar with the term 'dissertation' to describe this though, but this is simply a matter of terminology. Because we are staying away from telling you what your thesis should look like, how it should be specifically structured or what is should contain, this book should broadly apply to all discipline areas, and to full-time and part-time students alike.

Throughout the book we combine styles, offering you some advice from our experience, and at times taking a more non-directive coaching approach to helping you find your own way forward. Coaching is a professional partnership (in this case between you and us) which helps you to become more self-aware, access the resources around you and consciously decide and enact your own way forward. In this we expect you as the coachee to use your own judgement and make decisions about the best way forward for you, you; are the expert in your own life. We encourage you to do more of what works for you, and do less of what doesn't help you make progress. There's no one right way through the thesis writing process. All we ask is that you approach this book, and your thesis, with an open mind and be willing to try out new things.

Finally, we want to encourage you to use your limited time wisely. We do not advocate that you take time to read this book in one sitting, because you should be writing one! We would not insist that you read the book cover to cover. Nor do we offer you a guide packed full of academic references which will take you time to read, appraise and decipher. Please do dip in and dip out of the sections you need. On the same note, there are excellent blogs, further reading and other resources out there for academic writers, but don't delay your finished thesis by scouring the Internet for the magic tip that makes thesis writing easy. We have seen a number of people put off engaging with doing the writing in search of the mythical key to easy completion. The way to get to the end is to keep coming back to your writing practice and keep chipping away at your thesis.

Kay Guccione and Jerry Wellington

CHAPTER ONE

Writing as a partnered enterprise

The changing context of doing a doctorate

Without wishing to go too far back in history, it is worth outlining briefly how the context for doing a doctorate has changed radically in a relatively short time (two decades perhaps). Having an overview of these changes should help in seeing more clearly the current context in which doctoral students and their supervisors work. It also illustrates the constraints and the climate in which supervisors and students now collaborate in working towards a successful thesis – and therefore the demands which both 'sides' could and should make of each other (as we explore later in this chapter).

Very briefly, we can say that doctorates are now characterized by:

- Diversity not uniformity: there is an increased number and range of students with a range of ages, attendance patterns, background, 'class', location and origins. There is also a wide range of models and versions of the doctorate and modes of study available to students.

- Globalization: postgraduate study in the United Kingdom and elsewhere is subject to increasing influence and competition from Europe, the United States, South East Asia, Australia and other regions.

- Regulation: quality control, auditing and accountability are increasingly present at national and institutional levels.

- Growing utilitarianism, that is, increased concerns about utility and purpose for the 'knowledge economy', with a demand for the doctorate to inculcate 'generic skills', which may increase 'employability'.

- An increasingly different view of what learning, teaching and supervision are.

(For a more detailed discussion of these changes see, e.g. Taylor and Beasley 2005; Wellington 2010.)

These changes have led to a greatly altered view of what it means to be a student and an 'academic supervisor' in a university and, in turn, what it means to be 'supervised'. It could be said that the role of the supervisor has changed from one involving trust, professional pride, integrity, responsibility and autonomy ... but equally a context of laissez-faire ('leave the student and supervisor to get on with it'), supervision as a behind closed doors or secret garden process, and oral agreements to one involving a context of accountability, auditing, openness, guidelines, pressure, written recording of meetings, regular progress reporting, 'standards' and quality assurance.

This 'from-and-to' way of portraying the changed context is slightly caricatured, but it should be familiar to experienced supervisors or to students who are in their tenth year of doctoral study or longer. (We are partly joking here, but one of us recently supervised a PhD student who took twelve years of part-time study to complete her doctorate, and when asked why it took so long, she told us that she just 'enjoyed doing it'.) The arguments for increased regulation and scrutiny of doctoral work are numerous: It provides structure, frameworks and timelines; it should lead to equity and consistency; it makes clear and explicit the rights, responsibilities, roles and expectations of both student and supervisor; it provides a 'paper trail' of doctoral progress which can be valuable to both parties. Equally, we have seen strong arguments presented to show the dangers and disadvantages of increased control and scrutiny. For example, it can stifle creativity; it does not allow for flexible timing and leads to 'forced pacing' of the research and writing, as opposed perhaps to 'letting it flow'; it assumes 'linearity' in the doctoral 'journey' rather than the cyclical, more messy approach that characterizes real research; it is part of the general context of 'mass production' or massification in higher education.

We leave this section by showing Table 1.1 below for you to ponder on, showing some of these polarized viewpoints.

Table 1.1 Regulatory contexts: Have they led to standardization or improvement? Two sides of the story ...

Positive – for regulation	Negative
A timely end to laissez-faire, a 'behind closed doors' approach	Severe scrutiny, constant audit
Demise of the secret garden	Removed autonomy, stifled originality
Wise risk management	An end to risk ... managed mediocrity, squeezed creativity
Pragmatism, improved completion rates, emphasis on making the doctorate 'do-able'	Constant time keeping, closed-ended, excessive or unhelpful pressure to complete
End of unwanted risk-taking	Doctorates by numbers
Supervisor training improves completion rates	Supervisors cannot be trained – supervisor development is the aim (reflective practice)
Introduction of generic skills agenda to increase (for example) employability	Skills demand reduces completion rates. (It gets in the way of the doctoral contribution.)
Stress on 'getting it done' (it's not the Nobel Prize)	Stress on simply passing or meeting the Regulations Or getting it done – an increase in '1-0' victories to achieve the doctorate

No need to be alone: The importance of staying connected

Community spirit: It's probably not a surprise to you that your experience of learning how to do research and how to be a researcher in your field is influenced by the people around you, who to varying degrees can act as guides and teachers, help you interpret what's required of you to achieve scholarliness, give you feedback, include you in conversations about their own research work, and cheerlead for you. Sometimes these positive aspects of development are hard to access because you aren't located for most or all of the time in the same place as your department, because the people around you don't care to help you with these things, or because the people around you aren't aware of what you need from them. Then it can be hard to fully take on the identity of a researcher, and it can feel a bit fraudulent and frightening to be writing a book about your opinions on a specialist topic, especially a book you are going to be examined and judged on.

For a proportion of students, this anticipated process of becoming accepted into a community of scholarly peers has not happened for whatever reason, and they stay on the periphery of the academy feeling like they don't belong.

It's like I'm looking into a building through the windows of academia. I can understand what I see through each individual window, but I'm not part of it and I can't get the full picture. What else is in there that I can't see, what am I missing?

I've never really felt included, maybe I didn't include myself. I see others chatting away about their work and asking questions and I feel as if I never fully committed to my PhD. I was always afraid of looking amateurish, so I was standoffish with people, and at this end point I can't say I feel I've actually got there.

For others, the decision to pursue a doctorate was a strategic career development move. Professionals who work in another role throughout their doctorate perhaps remain anchored in that sense of self and not the academic version as it's not as important to them on a day to day basis. Researchers who came in to the doctorate in order to move on into an industry may not feel a pull towards the academic way of life, and are just here to get the degree and move to a new role.

> *I'm an architect really. I still have my business, and my clients, I get out and see what needs doing, I have to keep up with all my old memberships, and networks, and the magazines they send, because I will need them still when I've finished this. I have felt pulled to be more, and do more, but I need to still keep being myself, that's the core of who I am.*

> *I came in and I wanted to be in a job at a [biotechnology company] in 3 years, that was my limit and I promised myself that's what I'd do. So I've been really selective about what I spend time on. Does it get me that job? Yes I'll do it. Is it for academic debate and intellectual value only? No, it's not for me.*

We have seen these examples, and they are cited more as reasons for feeling distant from the research and having low confidence in writing. Students without a sense of belonging to a community that can support them variously describe themselves as being isolated, lost, clueless, adrift, at sea, alone and at the mercy of their fate. Talking about these experiences and connecting to others helps. And talking to others is not just a cathartic pursuit designed to maximize group commiserating. When we verbalize what we are thinking in order to communicate it to others, we have to create a sentence that isn't disconnected fragments. In processing our thoughts into a sentence that makes sense, we come to understand more about what we are thinking and feeling. This is the reasoning behind the one-to-one and group-mentoring approach to supporting writers. Some more benefits of talking things through with others are below, and in Chapter 4 we cover ways in which you can create a sense of community for yourself:

- You come to realize that feeling anxious about the thesis is common, it's a big challenge for most doctoral students.

- Getting insight from another point of view. We all have blind spots (biases in the way we think about ourselves), and so an external perspective can help us see them.

- Problems that seem large and complicated can be broken down into their component parts, then each of them can more easily be solved.

- You get validation of your ideas and choices. If someone else thinks it's a good idea, you have a frame of reference for the decision-making process.

- You are accountable to someone, and having them take an interest in your writing can help keep you on track.

- You have a person present to remind you of what you *can* do, and what you *have* achieved.

Spend more time with other students to keep a sense of perspective and break the isolation, and access more university support or resources – if nothing else, you meet other students on workshops you wouldn't normally see.

Support structures and communities: From private to public

One of the tangible benefits of the changes we highlighted earlier is that the traditional pedagogical model of a student working solely with her or his supervisor(s) is no longer tenable. We now have what might be called a form of distributed pedagogy in doctoral education. By moving from a one-to-one (or two) model of supervision towards a broader view of when and where doctoral education takes place, we see the importance of networks of learning in which students take the active role. Then, they are no longer passive recipients of supervision. The old apprenticeship model (or at least 'sitting by Nellie') becomes an anachronism, and the danger of a folie à deux is removed. We therefore need to consider all of the following 'sites' in which teaching and learning can take place and in which the thesis can be produced:

- The cohort effect, especially strong when cohorts of students all start at the same time as in many professional doctorates

- Peer learning, that is, critical friends, student-led seminars

- Peer support

- Conference presentations

- Families and friends

- Employer involvement in supervising and perhaps examining (esp. Professional Doctorates)

- University mentors

- Mentoring by existing students; buddies

- Doctoral development programmes and workshops (sometimes called research training programmes)

- Internet links, websites, social media

- Relationships or links with other staff; staff seminars

- Research environments (attachment to funded projects, research centres, etc.)

By seeing pedagogy in this way, we move from a focus on isolation, independence and autonomy to one of networking, socially situated learning and collaboration. Incidentally, this move should lead to a change of emphasis and culture in the university, shifting away from simply supervisor training (or development) towards a broader look at distributed doctoral pedagogy and how it can be improved.

A coaching approach: The power of dialogue and the learning conversation

What is coaching?

Coaching in its simplest form is a conversation between two people which emphasizes thinking and learning. It is more disciplined and structured than a simple chat, and uses conversational techniques designed to help add depth to the discussion and enable self-evaluation. The overall aim of a coaching conversation is to help the coachees identify what they want to achieve, and then look for a creative way to enable them to do that. A good coach will minimize the advising they do, and instead ask questions that spark critical thinking. They will listen deeply, they will encourage and support the coachees to craft their own way forward. Coaching is a piece of work that is done within conversations, not a magic fix for problems. It uses dialogue to help spark new ideas and thinking.

What is the Thesis Mentoring programme?

Much of the content of this book is derived from the experiences of the now over 350 participants on the Thesis Mentoring programme at the University of Sheffield. In this programme, thesis writers (mentees) are paired with a postdoctoral researcher (the mentor) who is trained to use coaching conversations and who helps their mentees focus on their approach to getting their thesis writing done. Over the course of sixteen weeks, the pairs discuss writing blocks and issues, identify options, and experiment with new ways of doing things, and craft new writing patterns and plans which work for each individual. The programme works on a foundation of creative problem solving, and critical thinking and is therefore well suited for use in the research environment.

What is solution-focused coaching?

For thesis writing, where there is a defined goal of a complete thesis, by a defined deadline, we prefer a solution-focused approach to coaching (Cavanagh and Grant 2010). The emphasis of this approach is in getting thesis mentees to imagine, discuss and move towards a 'desired future state', that is, a better way of being and feeling about their thesis and their doctorate. It is situated within an idea that events and their meanings are constructed through dialogue (constructivism), and talking about a situation in new ways and from different perspectives can change the way it is understood and experienced (O'Connell 1998). It avoids spending time recalling and deconstructing past histories, and instead moves from the present 'what is' to the imagined better future, via creative solutions.

What is self-coaching?

Although solution-focused coaching is most frequently done as a one-to-one conversation, we sometime use other approaches such as group workshops, peer-coaching and self-coaching. Groups and peers have the advantage that there is still an element of thinking out loud involved, perspectives and understanding can be compared, and vocalizing an issue is preferable to mulling it over in your own head.

Self-coaching is possible though, if you can be disciplined and you make time for it. You can use coaching techniques to appraise where you are now, define where you want to be and identify your own route to thesis submission. We recommend that as you go through the questions below, and through the rest of the ideas in this book, you externalize the conversation with yourself, perhaps in writing, by using drawing or mind mapping, in blog, tweet or diaries, or by thinking out loud. We have tried to use as many doctoral voices as we could, to illustrate different ideas and perspectives for you to consider.

EXERCISE: *A few self-coaching questions based in a solution-focused approach are below. Pick and choose from this menu to suit your situation and your preferences. Every time you are tempted to think about what won't work, or what you can't do, look for what will, could or might work, and what you can do.*

- What have you learnt so far about writing, and what is working well?
- What one thing have you achieved today, and what does that mean for your thesis?
- What does a 'good thesis writer' look like, and what do they do?
- What's the most important thing you have to do to get the thesis finished?
- What would make it more likely for you to take action to do that important thing?
- What's the first thing you're going to do today to get you closer to your finished thesis?
- Which parts of writing the thesis are least unpleasant for you?
- What resources do you have that you're not using?
- How will you get what you need?
- Who can support you to do this?
- What do you do that produces good results?
- What other options do you have?

- What's your big ambition after your doctorate?
- What about the doctorate makes you smile?
- What will it mean to you to achieve the doctorate?
- What else could you do?

What should – students (reasonably) expect from their supervisor?

We start this section on students' needs and expectations with two interesting comments from students on the start of their doctorate, the first using the rather unflattering metaphor of an 'old slipper':

> *My supervisor actually asked me at the start: 'How do you want me to supervise you?' And I thought that was brilliant. We did kind of negotiate how to work together and then worked at it. … It kind of feels like an old slipper now, it feels quite comfortable. I tend to set the agenda for the meetings, it's mainly me. Again, that's because I trust her and I know she's bothered about me.*

A second student used the metaphor of 'congruence' between one set of expectations and another:

> You need to clarify expectations at the beginning – what are the student's expectations, what are the supervisor's? Are they congruent – if not then where are the disparities and how do you address those? It is useful to develop a time frame and to write a timetable … and agreeing frequency of meetings, contact outside of meetings – can I phone up, pop in, e-mail …?

(Both taken from Wellington 2010)

In our discussions with students, we have come across a wide range of perceived needs, expectations and wants. It is worth noting at this point that a student's *wants* may be very different to a student's *needs* and we return to this later. To give the reader a flavour of these expectations, we offer a random list of examples, which contain a range of metaphors, a tendency which we examine in the next section: I want a hard worker; 'toughness'; good guidance and signposting; a critical friend; I want the 'voice of experience'; someone directive yet non-judgemental; someone who leaves space for my initiative; someone to trigger creativity; a good listener; cconsistency; openness and honesty (from both sides); respect; open to my perspective ... yet agenda-setting; instils confidence; is confident himself or herself; I don't want any surprises at the end!

In basic terms, we have found that students' expectations of supervision can be classified under four main categories:

1   Technical and organizational: For example, setting deadlines; 'where are you at?'; reminders; a quick response; not changing the goalposts; agreeing parameters.

2   Practical: for example, on aspects of writing; practical ideas on methods, access; regular contact; a balance between informal and formal contact.

3   Pastoral or affective: for example, praise; encouragement; empathy; support; tolerance: 'someone who will tolerate my ramblings'; a safety net (Am I doing OK?); interpersonal interaction; 'keeping me motivated'; supportive criticism; 'showing an interest'; reassurance.

4   Philosophical, theoretical, conceptual: for example, providing 'a road map'; keeping me focused or 'keeping me on track'; setting boundaries; 'spotting the gaps'; openness to new ideas; debate; clarifying things; pointers to the literature; highlighting different viewpoints; saving students from getting too 'caught up' in their studies to see and recognize different points of view.

A student – supervisor relationship for writing

In the course of our work with thesis writers, and in formal roles as Head of Research Degrees, we interact with many students who report how their relationship with their supervisor influences how they feel about their degree, their thesis, their data, the contribution they are making to their research field, and their future career path. We understand then that there is strong interplay between supervision and confidence and authority in writing. In fact it's very hard to finish your doctorate without your supervisor. You as a student stand to benefit from your supervisor's research experience and expertise, and the supervisor is the person best placed to give you feedback on the content and angle of the thesis. Sometimes though this key relationship is neglected, or strained, or just not as open as you'd like it to be. And the added tension of this can grind productivity to a halt, helping no one.

Student – supervisor relationships can exist in very varied structures: as dyads, within research groups, as large supervisory teams or thesis committees, with industrial or practice partners. Different institutions can have different rules, and roles they expect within supervisory arrangements and each can bring challenges. The tone and quality of the relationship between each individual student and each of their supervisors can also vary greatly, and it changes over time, and in response to the natural workload ebb and flow, the research environment, and the stressors of the doctorate. Doctoral students may describe their supervisory relationship as being akin to being close friends, as friendly colleagues, as professional acquaintances, as barely tolerable, or as unbearable. We aren't going to unpick the reasons why, or talk about what could have been; such pathology is probably not useful to you right now. What we want to say here, in a book intended for students in the final phases of the doctorate, is that whatever your current experience may be, there are steps you can take to ensure you and your supervisor are prepared for and in agreement about the plan for your thesis. In effect, there are ways in which you can manage your communications and how you relate to each other to minimize distraction from the primary goal of finishing. It's never too late to renegotiate a working relationship that will get you to the end – you have a mutual interest in getting the thesis finished and you can ally yourselves to get it done.

I'd fallen into patterns of being totally passive and letting communication difficulties just fester. If our relationship had stayed like it was, there's no way I would have been able to do it. It was horrible. Now we work to try to understand each other's perspectives, we're less passive-aggressive.

Try to establish clear boundaries and expectations with your supervisors and not let differences fester. It won't get better if you leave it.

Clashes in supervision are usually reported to have roots in personality differences, differences in our motives for being in the academic environment, a clashing work ethic, or mismatched communication styles or preferences. But consider that neither of you can change those things about the other person, and it's perfectly possible to have a productive working relationship with people with whom you do not share the same personality and style. Having clear boundaries, keeping communication channels open, and looking for ways in which you complement each other will help you ally yourselves towards the finish line.

Clarity is better than friendship – clear boundaries

Establishing some ground rules about working together can help even in the most strained supervisory arrangements. Let your supervisor(s) know you're committed to getting the thesis written, and that you want to find the best way to work together. What do you expect from each other? Where will the writing be done and how much time will you spend on it per week? Are there any other commitments or demands on anyone's time to be aware of? What's the turnaround time for submitting and receiving supervisory comments? How often will you meet? Are any of you going to be away travelling or on leave during this period? How do the rules change if one of you is away? What will you do if you get stuck? What do you need from each other in order to feel confident in getting to the end? Chapter 7 contains more on negotiating the feedback process.

> *In my experience, some supervisors are sensitive to the outside stresses that can affect a students' ability to complete their thesis, and work with them to minimize them. Other supervisors are less intuitive and we need to guide them.*

You have a Common Goal

It's a safe bet to say that it is in both (or all) of your interests that this doctorate, and thesis, should be completed on time. You have a shared goal here, and keeping this in mind, and reiterating it through all communications will keep you focused on working together. Some more things you and your supervisor(s) are likely to have in common are:

- You both have a full and pressured workload with deadlines and demands imposed by others that will affect the time you have available for each other.

- You like to feel secure that you know what's going on, and to be kept in the know about things that affect you.

- If you don't know about a problem or issue, you can't do anything about it.

- You don't want to find out about problems via someone else, or be gossiped about.

- You don't want to have assumptions made of you, or about you, you'd rather have people check the facts.

- You want to be told the truth, and knowing something upfront is better than finding it out too late.

- You don't want to be stood up, put off or cancelled at late notice.

You will be able to find more commonalities that fit your experience and situation. The idea behind looking for similarities rather than differences is that it creates a sense of perspective, and of empathy with the other person. You may have to work, and write hard, to cultivate this shared understanding, but it's a starting point for a better working relationship.

I've realized that I don't have to present the best version of myself to my supervisor. It is fair and good to actually tell him what I've been doing, about the progress I have made, even if the outcome is not what he expected ... instead of just not turning up as if I haven't got anything to show to him.

Open up communications

We have worked with several students who have not been in touch with their supervisor for a while, perhaps up to a year. Perhaps you've let things slide, cherishing being left alone to get on with it. Maybe you're uncertain where you stand with that person now, and feel foolish asking. Or did things end awkwardly last time you met and you're unsure of how to get back in touch? An email text you could adapt for getting back in touch is below:

Dear [supervisor(s)],

I am getting in touch as I am aware that my thesis deadline is approaching [date] and I want to do what I can to make sure that I am doing everything I can to submit on time.

I am aware that we have not been in touch since [date]:

and that last time we spoke things did not go well between us.

and that last time we spoke it was agreed that I would do [tasks], which I have not yet got back to you about.

and that I have missed the deadline we agreed for [tasks] and let myself and you down.

and that my progress has been slow, and I've not kept you properly informed of what I was doing.

I have reflected on this, and I can see that continuing on in this same way is going to be uncomfortable for both or all of us, and likely to waste both or all of our time and energy. Making sure we set off on this last phase in a better way is part of my commitment to completing on time.

I think we both stand to gain from a conversation where we make some basic agreements about how I will approach the writing and how I can keep in touch to make sure you are informed of progress. I would also like to know from you what time frames are appropriate to enable you to give me feedback on my writing, and if there are any busier times for you or times you are on leave and will be unavailable, so that I could plan accordingly.

What do you think? Could we meet or chat on the phone or Skype and agree a way that suits us both?

With thanks

[student]

Some of the conversations you have as you find a way of working together that works for you both are going to feel awkward. Don't let this discomfort put you off, it will save you more long-term discomfort if you put the effort in now. Being prepared for the conversation will help you get across what you want to say, and give you the capacity to listen to what is being said in response. A link to a downloadable planner for difficult conversations is here, as part of a suite of Thesis Planning tools that have been created for this book. http://www.sheffield.ac.uk/ris/ecr/mentoring/thesistools

I believe that if I was to do it all over again, one thing I would do differently would be to ask for help and let people know that I am stressed when I first start feeling stressed – instead of letting it build up to crisis point. In these final stages, I have now finally learnt to be more vocal.

Being ignored is not OK – what to do

We have seen unfortunate cases of students whose emails go unanswered and who cannot pin their supervisor down for face-to-face time to have feedback meetings. If you aren't getting appropriate responses, and allocated time for discussion by your supervisor(s), and you have already tried the above ideas, it's a good idea to raise this as an issue with the designated staff member for doctoral student matters in your department as soon as possible.

Harassment and bullying are not OK – what to do

Bullying and harassment of staff or students is against the law and is a very serious matter. Every institution will have policies for staff and students tackling the issue and advising what to do. Harassment in your doctorate from any person to any other is not acceptable in any circumstance and you do not have to put up with it. It is your responsibility to find a way to report it as soon as you can and seek support. Harassment is defined in the Equality Act (2010) as "unwanted conduct related to a relevant protected characteristic, which has the purpose or effect of violating an individual's dignity or creating an intimidating, hostile, degrading, humiliating, or offensive environment for that individual." Bullying can be defined as any behaviour, delivered in any form, that is malicious, insulting, offensive or intimidating, ranging from repeatedly ignoring a person or subjecting them to unwelcome attention, humiliation, ridicule or threats (ACAS, 2014). Bullying can also take the form of multiple or repeat episodes of behaviour which is trivial as a one-off event. Extreme forms of harassment and bullying include physical threats or violence but harassment and bullying may also be far more subtle. You do not have to put up with any form of harassment or bullying in the course of your doctoral study. Harassment or bullying may not always be intentional, but are always unacceptable, whether intentional or not. If you are experiencing this type of behaviour in the course of your degree, we urge you to get in touch with someone you trust in your own department or in the student services department of your university.

Metaphors for the supervisor and the doctoral 'journey'

Supervisors and students frequently use metaphors when they are asked to talk about the writing and supervision process and 'what they want' from it. Reflecting on these metaphors can be of great value in aiding our understanding of the mentoring and supervision process – and therefore improving practice.

For example, students often talk about being 'on track' or more negatively 'off track'. They see the supervisor's role as keeping them on track. We have come across a wide and unexpected range of metaphors in describing the 'journey' (itself a favourite metaphor). The supervisor is seen as: an anchor, keeping the ship stable in rough seas; a mirror, in reflecting back or bouncing back questions and issues to the student; and similarly, a sounding board. Guidance metaphors abound when students are asked to reflect on the supervisor's role: a guide over a mountain range, but not to carry your luggage for you; a satnav; an air traffic controller with the student in the cockpit. Equally, supervisors see themselves as a navigator, a companion on the doctoral journey, and commonly a critical 'friend' and a critical reader in later phases. More rarely, we have come across coaching metaphors as in:

I'm a bit like a tennis coach – you work on different aspects, it's one to one, you've got to help them with style, and they have to compete at the end – well, 'perform' anyway, in the viva. (Wellington 2010, 57)

Finally, other notions which have surfaced in discussion include those of someone leading the way, showing you where to go through the 'doctoral maze'; an adviser; a devil's advocate; a manager; a gate keeper; a holiday representative; a counsellor, like a marriage counsellor perhaps; a mentor and her or his apprentice (learning the 'craft of research'); a marriage between two partners; a parental relationship (maternal or paternal); the supervisor as a clock; and the supervisor as a scaffold.

Metaphors could be dismissed as 'just a way of seeing things', but that is exactly what they are. They can therefore be valuable in pondering on how the student, mentor, supervisor and others can best work together to produce a successful thesis. Perhaps the most widely cited text on the importance of metaphor is that of Lakoff and Johnson (1980), who argue that metaphorical language is not merely 'frilly speech' but is central in our thought processes, our understanding of the world and our expression of not only this understanding but also the way we feel about it, that is, the affective domain as well as the cognitive. Similarly, Cameron (2003) suggests that a metaphor often has an affective role, sometimes in expressing a view or a feeling more subtly in a metaphorical rather than a directly literal way (see Chapter 3 of this book); equally Kovecses (2000) argues that the use of metaphor is an important way of expressing feeling.

Another seminal text (Ortony 1993) has as its main thesis statement the argument that new understanding can be created when a metaphor is used and that metaphors offer a new way of viewing situations and processes (in the case of this book, thesis writing, mentoring and supervision). A focus on metaphor has also featured in a small number of studies of supervision. To take one example, Mackinnon (2004) suggested the metaphor of a 'fiduciary relationship' between supervisor and student, based on her own experience as a solicitor and a law academic.

We leave the last thought in this section to Lakoff and Johnson (1980, 239) who argue that 'metaphors are not merely things to be seen beyond. In fact, one can see beyond them only by using other metaphors.'

And finally ... a note on the word 'supervision'

It is worth noting that although the word 'supervision' is in common use, certainly in the UK, it is itself used metaphorically, and in some ways it has certain, perhaps unwanted, connotations. In many places the term 'adviser' is preferred. The verb 'to supervise' is related in most dictionaries to the verbs to oversee, to survey and to inspect. The noun 'supervisor' is sometimes defined as a person who 'exercises general direction or control over a business or a body of workmen' or as one 'who inspects and directs the work of others' (Shorter OED). Indeed, Lee and Green (2009, 626) argue that the very word 'super-vision' invites an excess of 'visual metaphors' including overseeing and what they call 'the authorised and authorising gaze of an already-established researcher'.

Many students and their supervisors would be very uncomfortable with the language of controlling, surveying, overseeing and inspecting; some would be more at ease with the idea of 'directing', but a delicate balance needs to be maintained between being 'left alone' and being 'directed' (Delamont et al. 1998; Wellington 2010, 42–60).

CHAPTER TWO

Writing milestones and crunch points

Writing as early as possible

We are aware that some of our readers for this book may be super-prepared and coming to read about 'getting to the end' at a much earlier stage of their doctorate unlike the people for whom most of the book is written. This is great news – it will not hurt you at all to read this now! As added value for you, we wanted to use this short chapter to give you some steer on writing now, while there is plenty of time. From the beginning of the doctorate, there is writing you can be planning, drafting and completing. A good foundation in academic writing, and being prepared to flex and review, makes for a far easier time of writing the thesis later, and the more you can do as you go, the better for you. We do not agree that 'doing' research and writing research should be separate endeavours and contest the idea that an endpoint 'writing up' phase is a good way to manage the doctorate.

In addition, you will have picked up our repeated mantra that we encourage you to get started with writing as soon as possible. Please let this sink in; we really mean it, and perhaps even take a few minutes of today to think about how you can get started with writing as a matter of development, and in refining your thinking about your research and what it is already showing you (see Chapter 3 for more on the partnered processes of writing and thinking). Take some time to read through the student voices woven into this book and listen to the messages they convey about getting started, and how they wish they had done it earlier. If you won't believe us, maybe they can convince you.

So to the doctoral milestones and crunch points, you can think about now, and that will make your future writing life easier. Each stage of the doctorate involves different activities, styles of thinking, types of writing and needs for advice and supervision.

Drafting your research proposal

There is a high probability that if you are from a science, engineering, maths or medicine discipline, this proposal document has already been prepared in order to gain funding for the project you are doing or are about to do – the 'grant proposal'. If your research proposal is already written, and your project already funded, you could think about skipping to the confirmation review section. But before you race ahead, consider that this section may be worth a read through anyway, as it could provide you with some insight into how research questions and research proposals are developed. It could give you some context about the problem you are trying to solve, and the wider field it's situated within. There are advantages in having it already done for you – yes, in that you don't have to take the time to write it yourself. But consider, you have also missed out on the deep thinking that goes into piecing together the proposal, setting your planned work within the literature base, and understanding why the methods were selected. At the very least, do make sure that you have a copy of the proposal that was written for your project, and that you have had the opportunity to digest, discuss and understand the framing of the work you are undertaking. If you can, discuss with the writer – likely to be your supervisor(s) – their thinking in developing the proposal. This will give you insight into how good research questions and plans are developed, and can only help inform your approach to structuring your thesis and your arguments within it.

One of the earliest, but unfortunately the hardest, tasks is to write a clear research proposal; the difficulties with writing initial proposals are 'well recognised' (Cryer 2000, 21). To a large extent within the arts, humanities, and social sciences disciplines, prospective students have to do this at a very early stage in order to apply for and be accepted onto a research degree programme. This is especially true for the MPhil or PhD programme. For many professional doctorates, the job of writing a research proposal may be the final written assignment in the 'taught' element. It would be unfair to make one of the admission criteria for a PhD the production of a perfectly formed research proposal, with clearly formulated research questions, stating exactly what is to be done and when, how data are to be collected and analysed, which ethical issues will arise, what the literature base will be, and how the study will make a contribution to knowledge in the field. Those may well be the criteria for a finished thesis, but real-world research is far too unpredictable and 'messy' for the perfectly polished proposal to be an admission requirement. Our view is that the research proposal should show good potential and admit that certain aspects of the study, for example, gaining access to people or resources, deciding on the sample size, and developing a method, will have to be determined as part of the process.

We suggest that the initial proposal should address, at least, the following twelve questions:

1   What is my provisional title?

2   What area or field am I investigating or working in?

3   Why is this topic or area important? Why have I decided to study this?

4   What are my main research questions? Where did these 'come' from?

5   What has been done in this area already? That is, an outline, at least, of the likely literature base.

6   What is the context for the study? For example, global, national, institutional or personal.

7   What theory, theories or theoretical framework can I draw upon?

8   What is the proposed methodology? Why? And which specific methods are likely to be used? Why these and not others?

9   For an empirical study, how will the sample be determined?

10   What issues are likely to emerge around: (a) access to people, equipment and resources? (b) Are there ethical considerations in the course of the research?

11 How will data be analysed (whether primary or secondary data)?

12 What timescale, approximately, will I try to follow – and is it humanly possible?

And finally, ask yourself: How many theses will I be writing? The answer to this question should always be one – keep it manageable!

Our experience is that proposals are often said to be 'good' or 'strong' if they have most of the characteristics shown under the following five categories. Many of the terms used below will need unpacking or operationalizing in order to give them meaning, for example, 'critical engagement', 'appropriate methodology' (see Chapters 5 and 6 for our discussion of these and other terms). These criteria will also be useful to you if you are at the stage of producing an end-of-first-year 'confirmation' or 'upgrade' report. If you are a student in the final stages of the doctorate, and you are still reading, you can use the information below to shape and refine your ideas for your thesis.

Focus

- The research questions are clearly laid out and focused with clear boundaries.

- The research questions are not too ambitious, wide-ranging or optimistic.

Methodology

- The methodology should be appropriate, that is, clear about what will actually be done and why.

- It should be very doable, not relying on too many unknowns or potential points of failure.

- Access to resources, people and equipment have been considered.

- Ethical issues have been considered, and permissions needed acknowledged.

- Examples of potential methods or tools have been included.
- It should give some indication of how the data are to be analysed.

Summary of the literature base

- The proposed study is located in existing literature and is set in its historical and methodological context
- Detailed, well-reviewed
- Shows 'critical engagement' and understanding of the salient issues, goes beyond a simple description of the literature
- Provides a comprehensive literature base
- Critical reflection on the policy context (if appropriate)

Theoretical framework or conceptual clarification

Shows theoretical clarity
Research questions located within a theoretical framework

General

It has the potential to make an original contribution to the field
Generally it has potential, mileage, currency or scope.

Refining the proposal, making it doable

No research proposal can be perfectly polished or focused at the outset. Indeed, the main purpose of the early stages of supervision is for you to work with your supervisor on achieving more clarity, interpreting early data, improving the research design and, not least, making it doable and manageable. This is a demanding job and will take time – in many cases, a clearer focus may not even emerge until you have considerable empirical work completed, and have begun to see what can or cannot be done. It is a constant process of thinking, refining, going back, checking and sometimes making guesses and taking chances. The essence of the doctorate is in making the unknown known; so don't panic if your neatly laid-out proposal needs to be adapted and crafted further. As the Nobel Prize-winning scientist Sir Peter Medawar described it, scientific method is a 'mixture of guesswork and checkwork' (Medawar 1963, 1976). Thus the research process is not a linear one, but is cyclical or iterative. Your writing can be viewed in this way too: What you write first won't be what you finally submit in your thesis, but continual writing will help refine your ideas and plans in an ongoing way (see Wellington, 2010, for a fuller account of 'weaving the threads' of your research).

We urge you to view the document you have created or received as a live piece of work. What we mean by this is that once created, it will help you to keep it somewhere accessible (e.g. computer desktop rather than buried in a folder you forget about) and revisit it regularly as your thinking and your project develops. Adding to this live document each time you read new literature, and therefore coming to know more about your subject area will help you build a string foundation for the literature review to come. Adding a list of the experimental or data collection work you have done will help you track your progress, and gain a handle on what your work in progress is showing you. New methodologies and methods can be added as you adapt techniques and refine your protocols, schedules or scripts. You can see where we are going with this; a continual banking of small pieces of writing is going to help you immensely with the next writing tasks: your confirmation review, any publications arising from the research, and with the final thesis.

Another early milestone: The confirmation review

For all doctoral students, one of the early challenges is to pass through what is often called the 'confirmation review' (also called the 'progress review' or 'first year *viva*' in some universities and formerly referred to as the 'upgrade' or 'upgrade review'). Normally, full-time students will undergo their review by the end of their first year of study; for part-time students it may be before or around the end of year 2.

Why do doctoral programmes have these checkpoints?

The main purpose of the confirmation review (CR) is to show that your work is making progress and that it has enough promise, substance and 'mileage' to lead to a doctorate. The other, secondary though important, purposes of the CR are: first, to give you practice in being asked questions about your work so far in a face-to-face situation – this is in some ways a practice for your final *viva* although, as we see shortly, some of the questions will be of a different nature; the second purpose is to allow both you and your supervisors the opportunity to present your proposed research, and the work done on it so far, to a fresh pair of eyes. This always, in our experience, leads to valuable feedback. The staff involved in the CR should give formative feedback and guidance to the student on (for example) her or his: writing; oral presentation; literature coverage; methodology; ethical issues; scope and focus; and future plans and timetable. The CR process also provides valuable feedback to supervisors – it may well be the first time that the student and supervisors have 'gone public' and opened out their work to a new audience for comment and helpful criticism.

Preparing for the CR

The initial challenge for the student, with her or his supervisors' help, is to produce a well-written progress, confirmation or upgrade report or paper for the (usually) two reviewers to examine prior to the *viva*. Most CR papers are around 10,000 words in length and will usually contain at least the following elements (check your own university regulations to be sure you are preparing the right thing.):

1 Some discussion of the existing literature in the area and its importance to the proposed study. This is not meant to be the final version but students must demonstrate that they have a good grasp of key literature in the area, even if they are not yet fully engaged with all the arguments.

2   The aims of the study, stated as clearly as possible; the paper should include some discussion of the methodology including theoretical and analytical frameworks which are to be used. At this stage, students may still be clarifying their focus.

3   Some discussion of the proposed methods of study and ethical issues.

4   Full references to research and secondary sources which have been used as well as those still to be accessed.

5   A draft structure for the final thesis, including chapter headings and a short summary of content for each chapter.

6   A timetable for the study including an estimate of likely completion date.

7   Any questions that the student would like to pose to reviewers during the *viva*.

The CR *viva*: What might be asked?

Two suitable reviewers are chosen by the supervisors in consultation (we suggest) with the student. These reviewers will need adequate time to read the paper and then jointly prepare for the *viva*. We cannot predict the specific questions they are likely to pose, so do ask your supervisor to discuss this with you. Bear in mind there is no prescribed set of questions – this is part of the unpredictability of all *vivas*, as we discuss in Chapter 9. However, we think the general questions they are likely to ask might, and perhaps should, include (again be aware of discipline differences in data collection and analysis methods) the ones listed below.

General

● Motivation: Why do you want to do this piece of research? Why did you choose this topic? Why do you think it is important?

● Position: What is your own position (professional or personal) in relation to this field and these research questions? What prior conceptions and/or experiences will you bring to this study and how are these likely to affect your data analysis and data collection?

● Contribution: Could you summarize your likely thesis? What might somebody from this field learn from reading your thesis that they haven't known before? What will you learn from doing it? What contribution do you hope to make?

Research questions

● What are the main research questions that you plan to address in your work? What was the origin of these questions?

Theories and theoretical frameworks

● What theories or theoretical frameworks or perspectives will you draw upon in your research? Why these and not others?

Literature review

● What has shaped or guided your literature review so far? Why has it covered the areas that it has? Why have other areas not been covered?

Methodology and data analysis

● Methodology: What methods do you plan to use? Why not others, for example, X? What will inform your choice of methods?

● Ethical issues: Which ethical issues do you expect to encounter: before, during and after your research?

● Your proposed sample characteristics and size: Why did you select this sample? Can you see any problems with it? If it is a small-scale study, can you justify why so few have been involved? (Note that these questions are likely to differ significantly across discipline areas.)

● Data analysis: How will you analyse your data? What packages or programmes will you use? What date-coding methods? What statistical analyses? Will themes emerge from your data (*a posteriori*) or will you 'bring them to the data' (*a priori*)? Why did you plan to analyse in this way? Could it be done in another way? (Again, note that these questions are likely to differ significantly across discipline areas.)

These possible *viva* questions are adapted from Wellington et al (2005, page 185) and we return to them in more detail in chapter 9.

The research timeline

● Is it realistic? How far are you along the way?

How should students behave in the *viva*?

Firstly, remember that this process and milestone are there to help you to progress. It is largely formative, more so than the final *viva*, although as the outcomes below show, it is partly about making

Table 2.1 Do's and Don'ts before and during the confirmation report *viva*

Don't	Do
Be dogmatic	Be thoughtful and reflective
Be defensive	Be honest
Be rude	Be direct, but not rude
Be long-winded	Be concise and specific (but don't give one word answers)
Try to please reviewers by contriving to include their work in the references	Carry out some 'homework' on the reviewers, their work and preferences
Be 'laid back' and blasé; think about your 'body language' and the overall impression you are giving	Be prepared, but not over-prepared e.g. by trying to predict *specific* questions

forward decisions. So expect to gain new learning, feedback and things to go away and think about as well as having the opportunity to share what you know. It's a good plan to revisit your CR document and add new thinking and feedback you receive in the CR *viva*. Again we urge you to view the document you have created for this checkpoint as a live document you can keep adding to.

The general behaviour that we advocate in Chapter 9 will also apply to this important live event. Treat it as a way of improving your doctorate and you are on to a winner. Here is our list of 'do's and don'ts', first published in Wellington et al. (2005, p. 194). Probably the main two are: do not be defensive; be confident without being arrogant. And try to enjoy it!

In short, use it as a unique learning process. It may be the best one that you have.

Finally, try to avoid going into your CR *viva* with a black eye picked up when playing basketball as one of this book's authors did (KG) – she was later asked why she came in with such strange make up. But all was well that ended well.

Possible outcomes

These vary from one university to another, but the most likely outcomes of the review will be to:

- Proceed with your doctorate, taking on board the feedback from the reviewers.

- Make amendments to your upgrade paper according to the recommendations of your reviewers: this may entail another *viva*, or it may not.

- Be asked to submit a fully revised version of the CR paper, perhaps with another *viva* to follow.

Please note that most universities do give the student a second chance if needed.

Writing through the doctorate

It seems like a statement of the obvious, but we feel there are three phases in the writing which take place to complete a doctorate.

Producing the CR paper is clearly part of the first phase and is a vitally important part of the 'journey'. (Sorry, we had to use this metaphor at least once). Each phase has its own characteristics.

Phase 1: Getting started

It is characterized by: becoming clearer about your title and research topic; focusing down, sorting out the scope and boundaries, drawing a line round your project, making it doable. Refining and focusing your research questions; developing a conceptual framework: What theories or theorists are you likely to use? Writing your methods, methodologies or materials and methods sections. Getting into a working routine, developing a writing routine and sorting out your personal time management; getting clear about your methodology and methods; making plans for data collection, for example, sample, gaining access, timing, ethical issues; doing some early reading and writing; and forming a working relationship and a pattern with your supervisor, including a system for record-keeping. Identifying your development needs as a researcher, and seeking to fulfil them. Ask all the questions you can; get the information you need, ask people why, and how and what.

Phase 2: The middle bit

It is characterized by: data collection; early data analysis; critical reading and writing around the literature; building up your references; keeping regular contact with supervisor; keeping records of supervision, either online or face-to-face contacts; building your professional networks; using other support systems such as writing courses, groups, retreats, workshops or buddies; writing chunks or drafting chapters and getting regular feedback on your writing from your supervisor; overcoming obstacles. Perhaps presenting at conferences, contributing to publications. Continued development of research and academic practices and skills sets; keeping your eye on what is needed for your future career, wherever that may take you. If you have lingering unknowns, go and get answers now. Talk to others, ask your supervisor, Google it!

Phase 3: The home strait

It is characterized by: finishing data analysis; keeping regular contact with peers and supervisor; developing your professional networks widely, continued reading and writing; presenting at conferences, developing oral skills for the *viva*; writing the concluding chapters, the discussion and the implications (the 'so what?' of your study); completing a first full thesis draft for someone to comment on (who?); completing the final thesis; final proof reading and polishing its presentation; continued development of research and academic practices and skills sets; taking steps towards applying for and securing your next role in your career path; discussing examiners; preparing for the *viva*. For more on the *viva* see Chapter 9.

The early stages – what you can do now?

From the above it looks as if there is a lot to do – and very often all at the same time. Don't panic, it's very doable. In terms of your forthcoming needs and the resources you want to be able to draw on during your doctorate, and to make sure your writing goes as well as it can, some things you can be finding out about to stand you in good stead for the future include the below points.

- Does your department have a 'postgraduate tutor' or head of research degrees who oversees supervision and may be someone to turn to for extra help, a second opinion, pastoral advice or support? Who is this person and how can you access them?

- Is the department used to working with a wide diversity of students for example, part-time students, mature professionals, overseas students, students who will need supervising 'at a distance', and are there peer groups you can join, or designated professionals who can help you with matters related to these demographics?

- How is your relationship with your supervisors going? Does their style of supervision suit your way of working?

Are you getting what you need? Are they accessible and able to give time to discussing your work and your writing? Have you made any assumptions about supervision, who will do what, whose responsibility, whose role? Check out your understanding and get clarity on what is expected of you.

● What other support structures are available to you as a doctoral student? What committees can you get involved with? What professional development programmes or workshops can you access at your university or through your funder? What groups or communities can help support your writing? What mentoring programmes can you access? What specialist services are available if and when you need them (e.g. Careers Support, Learning & Teaching Services, Disability Support, English Language Support, Counselling Support)? What's available online? What social media resources are there? What learning resources can be accessed anywhere any time?

The department and the individual supervisor(s) are important for a smooth passage through the doctorate, but the wider university context of regulations for supporting doctoral students' needs are to be looked into with equal care. Utilize everything you can to make sure your route through the doctorate is as smooth and supported as possible.

First steps in doctoral writing

A good way of getting started is to make a small start with a short, achievable piece of writing, with a mutually agreed deadline. It might be 1,000 words discussing a journal article, for example, a development that will count towards your literature review. This could be shared, in a friendly context, with your supervisor(s) and can form the focus of an early discussion, or perhaps with others in your research group or department. This not only gives you a feel of 'having started' but also gives you and your supervisor an early 'feel' for the processes of doctoral work, writing and feedback. This process involves reading, writing, drafting, getting feedback, making changes, redrafting and so on in a cycle. In these early stages the process is a more developmental one than it will be at later stages when writing will need feedback from new audiences and as students start to write for wider audiences. The general aim of inducting students into the writing process – and learning, or relearning the rules, conventions and traditions of scholarly writing – is an important goal in these early stages. Continue it through the doctorate. If you are nearer the end of your doctorate, this process is going to be compacted into a shorter space of time, so make sure any writing you do is focused towards what you will submit in your thesis.

In Chapter 3 we look at the connected, partnered processes of writing and thinking.

CHAPTER THREE

The parallel processes of research doing and research writing

What you need to know about getting started

I'm struggling to start writing my thesis and my stress levels are increasing as the days tick away.

We have talked to a lot of thesis writers, or would-be thesis writers, about how they approach getting started with writing and about what stops them from starting. In particular we like to ask people how they knew it was time for them to start writing. Sometimes this comes from an intrinsic sense that it's time, sometimes via a direct signal from the supervisor that it's time to start writing, and sometimes the pressure of the deadline means that, like it or not, it's time to start writing. Without a clear steer, or deadline pressure though, how do students motivate themselves to get started as soon as possible, rather than waiting for the direct order to appear as time ticks away. What happens if you wait too long to be told it's time to start? There are discipline differences in when it is 'normal' to start writing, but one thing we recommend for everyone is working on writing little and often, and beginning as soon as possible.

I was blissfully unaware how long it would take me to write up. To be honest I would have preferred a more clear marker from my supervisor, or from the department, saying stop doing experiments now and write! I was expecting someone to say when I had enough data, because I never felt I did, so instead I kept going much longer than I needed in the lab because I didn't know how much was enough. I feel pretty annoyed about that.

If there had been a requirement to hand in writing, and to have different pieces ready at different markers through the PhD, I would absolutely have done it. But you fall in with what others you see around you are doing, and you leave it all too late. I ended up putting most of a year of writing on credit cards because they stopped paying me at 3 years.

You are so torn at the end of the PhD, there ends up so much to do. Being able to get a job is really important yes, so filling in the applications will take some time up. Or if you're trying to get a grant to stay in your department, you need data for that, and to write it too. Your papers are important because you need them to even be considered for a job. And keeping up with your field is important; conferences don't wait for you to finish writing. You can distract yourself feeling you MUST do the other things. But if you never write your thesis because you're doing all that ... there's no point even doing the other stuff, you aren't going anywhere.

Through these student voice examples, you can see that for some students, there is no light-bulb moment where they suddenly experience a sense of 'readiness' to start writing. Many of the students we have worked with have stated this as an expectation – they assumed they would feel ready at some point, or were waiting to feel ready to start, before getting started. From other conversations we pick up other assumptions, stories people are telling themselves about their thesis, for example:

I'm not ready yet; I'm not good enough; I don't know how; I don't have enough data; I haven't got time right now; there's plenty of time left; it's not important right now; I'm not allowed to start yet; it's not normal to write now; I don't want to look too keen; I mustn't rush it; everyone else does it this way; I need to do 'x' first; If I do it too early I'll have to rewrite it ... etc.

EXERCISE: *Think about the messages about getting started with thesis writing you have picked up from the environment around you, and the messages you are reinforcing to yourself. Now write answers to these questions (1) What assumption are you making about starting thesis writing? (2) What are the consequences of this on getting your thesis finished on time?*

We certainly don't suggest that you drop everything in your research and home life, and concentrate solely on thesis writing to the detriment of other deadlines. It's an idea though to build up frequent small writing bursts that fit in and around other things, and that contribute piecemeal to the finished product. Some ideas about getting started with your thesis that you can enact today:

You know, everyone finds writing hard, but as you become more proficient, you learn about the way you work. You don't have to make the same mistakes over and over again, and you get quicker.

There's no right place to start

There's no set order you have to write the sections in, so the right place to start for you is on the section you will be able to get going on. Some people like to tackle the descriptive parts first – the materials, procedures and methods. Some people like to make themselves templates to write into, one per chapter with headings and formatting laid out to fill in piece by piece. Some construct figures or tables of their findings, describe them and then expand from their own data outwards. Others may prefer telling the story from the beginning, introducing each data chapter, presenting the data and then discussing it. Go with what works. What others did is not necessarily the best way for you.

Get yourself organized

If you haven't already, now is the time to get your data organized so you know where it all is and what it shows. Get all your papers together and make sure they are all catalogued in a reference manager. Tag, file and label accordingly. Beware of spending a long time getting this perfect! Don't let it become another thing you have to do before you start writing. The emphasis is on generating text, not having the most beautiful complex system of colour-coded organization.

Since it takes me a while to psych myself into writing, I am in habit of saying I need a certain period of time exclusively for writing or I can't do it at all. I am aware that I am not really making the most of each small amount of time here and there and that's time wasted.

Weave writing into your week

Don't tell yourself you need to wait for a free week to get started, that free week will never arrive. We'd argue you don't even need to wait for a free day. If you review your schedule week by week, you will be able to identify time slots of 30 minutes to 2 hours throughout the week in which to write in a short burst. If you are writing at home and caring for others, can anyone you know help you out for an hour or two a week? Or could you write responsively when your other responsibilities allow for it, having everything ready to go each time a small window of opportunity presents itself?

Breaking my work into small measurable tasks helped me to push myself from zero productivity, to doing the minimum work required per day, progress. This was easier to do on the bad days, and I did more than the minimum on the good days.

Plain language

Map out, or sketch out, or list what your data show and what you want to say in your thesis in plain everyday language first. What are the main things you want people to understand about the work you have done, what you found and what you recommend next. Make sure you solidly understand the contribution you are making first, then add the appropriate academic style and vocabulary of your research discipline. If you feel you are getting off track, or getting lost in the data, come back to these plain language versions of your key points.

Don't start from nothing

A good way to generate some draft text quickly is to take the top five articles off your desk, read each quickly, and then write one sentence to summarize what is important and original about that article. Then, without stopping to edit your work, expand each sentence into three sentences about that paper. Then check back if what you wrote is accurate. Then repeat the cycle of read–summarize–expand–check. Each section can then be copy/pasted to the appropriate subheading in your working documents.

No dead documents

Once you have completed some writing, for example, for your confirmation review (may also be called the PhD upgrade, mini-thesis, or the first year *viva*), for assessed components of your doctorate, or for an article or conference paper, keep them going. Save a copy as a 'live' or working document in an easily accessible file or app and revisit it as often as you can to add to it. Keeping your work(s) in progress visible makes it easy to drop in a couple of thoughts, ideas, notes about your reading, or things to follow up. Each time you read something, write something. Each time you complete something, write about it. Each time you have a new idea, get it written down. And don't forget to back this document up!

Don't delete dissatisfactory text

If you delete your writing, you'll regret it later. It's hard to say you've actually started writing if you are in a cycle of writing a paragraph and then deleting it. If you feel the mess is getting to you, and you have to tidy up your documents, try moving the offending text to a 'rough work' file. It may look to you now as if it's not up to standard, but with work you could refine these ideas and you don't want to have to redo this work. Don't get hung up on producing a perfect product first time, spare a thought for the processes of writing. You have to write draft one to iteratively move towards draft five. You are very likely to end up with written sections that do not make your final version, that's normal and not a waste of time at all. Deciding what to include, what to cut, what's relevant and what isn't, is all part of the critical process central to doctoral work.

> *I'm unwilling to settle for anything and can't seem to just get work done which is of a quality I'm happy with, hence my draft is now 4 months overdue.*

Find a place to be where you can write

You may find that just blocking out time works well for you. If you find you aren't able to prioritize writing in your everyday space though, removing yourself from your normal working environment and distractions could help. Find a new space you can keep just for writing. That might be taking yourself into a quite space such as another room in your house, a library or study space, or booking a meeting room. Or perhaps take yourself out for a coffee and an hour in a cafe environment a couple of times a week.

> *I don't really feel the space provided by my department for PhD students is very conducive to productive thesis writing, as they have now moved most PGRs into one room. I think the space I have for writing has a huge impact on how well I can focus on it, so I just go elsewhere.*

Knowing is not the same as doing

There's no golden tip you can read about which substitutes for actually sitting down and building up a daily practice of writing. The most important thing is to find a way to get started and work with that to expand your discipline, and your word count.

EXERCISE: *Take five minutes now to roughly map out what you can do today to get started (or get restarted) with thesis writing. Plan yourself about a thirty minutes task. Then go and do the task!*

Finding and nurturing your own motivation to write

A lot of the advice around setting effective goals and plans you can achieve asks you to set goals for your writing (or other tasks) which you are excited about or motivated by, arguing that you just won't stick to the goals which have no point to them, or which you subconsciously know to be unrealistic. If we know that a plan is futile, or pointless, we subconsciously put less effort in to following it. Putting less effort in decreases the likelihood of success. So how can we create a writing plan for ourselves which we are motivated to put our energy and effort into?

Writing a doctoral thesis doesn't always leave room for creativity and interpretation of the written format and style. There are likely to be limited opportunities for you to tailor your thesis writing into a style and end product which you find exciting. You need to comply with the conventions of your research field and with the guidelines your university provides for thesis writers. However much contributing to new knowledge is a creative process, there are still conventions to be followed and figure legends to be formatted appropriately.

I am recognizing through my many conversations with thesis writers that for a good proportion of you, the intrinsic motivator, the thrill of answering the research question, may be waning, or perhaps the excitement of engaging with research has passed altogether. How can you manage to find motivation to write when you are tired of your subject matter, when you've fallen out of love with the theories or if you've run out of energy for the analysis?

After 3 years I feel I have lost my motivation because academia is absolutely not what I thought it was. I want to finish the thesis as soon as possible so I can rethink my future, and move to a better suited place to work.

Don't worry about this. Recognize that for many of us projects are always more exciting at the beginning than in the middle or at the end. Remind yourself regularly what you gain from completing your thesis, and from completing your PhD. There are many things beyond the amazing sense of having contributed to global understanding, and of making an original contribution to knowledge. Find out what works for you and helps you reconnect with a sense of motivation and excitement about getting to the finish line, do any of the following appeal?

EXERCISE: *Which of these things motivate you a lot, a bit or not at all.*
I am looking forward to:

- *Putting my research experiences and expertise into practice in my next role*

- *Meeting new people in a new job*

- *Reconnecting with hobbies and interests I have put on hold to finish my doctorate*

- *Leaving behind colleagues who take a lot of energy to manage and work with*

- *Just really enjoying doing the writing*

- *A sense of completion and closure of a long and complex process*

- *Being known for the good research I have done, and sharing my achievements*

- *Seeing my research recommendations making a real world difference*

- *Moving to a new city, or back to my home city*

- *Introducing myself as Dr, and changing my bank cards to reflect my new title*

- *Writing my thesis in record time, faster than others*

- *The feeling of drawing a line under my doctoral experience and having the opportunity to start again*

- *Having more time to myself, to spend on whatever I choose*
- *Moving on to write articles and promote my work more widely*
- *Getting a job or promotion and earning more money*
- *Having more energy and finding more joy in life*
- *A sense of succeeding through a difficult process, and overcoming challenges*
- *A holiday or a travel break*
- *Moving my research into its next phase, taking the next steps in finding out more*
- *A career change, translating my experiences into a new context that is more suited to me*
- *Beating my own daily or weekly word targets*
- *Beating my colleague's daily or weekly word targets*
- *Being the kind of person who can be said to get things done*
- *The satisfaction of pushing myself to succeed with tasks that I'm not enjoying, gaining a useful life skill*

Find a way to remind yourself daily of what you gain by working on and finishing the thesis – set your computer desktop picture or your phone lock screen to remind you of your motivators, set calendar alerts, or head your To-do Lists with reminders of why you are doing this, and what you stand to gain.

What's the best motivator for writing your thesis? The one that works for you.

The emotional side of writing: 'more than a matter of cognition'

There is more to writing than simply skill, knowledge and ability, that is, cognition. This section discusses the importance of the 'affective domain' in completing a successful thesis. The origin of 'domains' in learning is usually attributed to 'Bloom's taxonomy' (Bloom 1956) – a classification which was developed in the 1950s and which experienced something of a revival at the start of the twenty-first century. The taxonomy involved three domains: the cognitive, the affective and the psychomotor. The affective domain is the component of Bloom's taxonomy which involves the feeling and emotional side of an activity, that is, enjoyment, motivation, drive, passion, enthusiasm and inspiration (Krathwohl et al. 1964).

Although a number of valuable articles on writing have been published over the last twenty years (e.g. Lea and Street 1998; Aitchison and Lee 2006; Bharuthram and McKenna 2006), relatively few have addressed the affective domain and the personal difficulties that students and other writers perceive and experience in writing (exceptions are Nightingale (1988) on problems; Lillis and Turner (2001) on confusions and concerns; Lillis (2001) on 'desire' and the self in academic writing). Prior to that, Ivanic's (1998) account of the relationship between academic writing and identity was one of the landmarks in the field.

Greater attention is now being paid to the role of emotion in education in the area of student writing (e.g. Lillis and Turner 2001). An extensive set of studies by Torrance et al in the 1990s (1992, 1994) looked at various aspects of students' writing, including the 'difficulties' they reported in a questionnaire. Many of these were located in emotional aspects of writing. We all know from experience that writing involves a great deal of cognitive energy. But for most if not all people, writing is also an experience that involves strong feelings and emotions: joy, pain, pleasure, frustration, enjoyment, angst, annoyance, relief and stress. The affective domain in writing is important and is therefore worth exploring and discussing, with the aim of helping you to recognize it, to manage it and to improve your relationship with writing by doing so.

One of the most emotional aspects of the process of writing a thesis or an article is the business of awaiting, anticipating, fearing and then receiving feedback on writing (on this and other aspects of feedback see Caffarella and Barnett 2000; Chanock 2000; Hyatt 2005; Värlander 2008), and we cover practicalities of feedback seeking later in Chapter 7. 'Timely and useful feedback on writing is hard to give and hard to take' (Wolcott 1990: 43).

What do students say about the emotional side of writing?

Based on a research study involving focus groups of students engaged in writing their theses (fully reported in Wellington 2010), we can summarize the main negative and positive views and feelings that students express.

The negative side of emotions in writing

When students are asked to reflect on their negative attitudes and feelings towards the activity of writing, they express a variety of comments and reflections.

Feelings of frustration and 'hard work'

Comments from students include such terms as 'cumbersome', 'torture', 'energy-sapping' and 'time-consuming'.

> *It is painstaking – I have tonnes of stuff in my head but can't put it into words.*

Getting started

From the previous sections in this chapter, you will realize that this is one of the most common areas where students express negative feelings and anxiety. It was sometimes a case of not knowing when to stop reading and when to start writing, or occasionally the problem of facing a blank screen. For example, students comment on:

- Worrying about getting started, where, when and how
- Having too many thoughts and getting bogged down with them
- First attempts at writing which are weak

- Knowing when to stop reading and balancing reading and writing
- Having a blank brain and seeing a blank screen in front of me

I feel as if I need to know everything first.

Feelings of pressure, fear and anxiety

Many students talk of emotions which include stress, fear and anxiety (covered more in Chapter 7):

- Pressure to be correct or get it right
- Feelings which vary according to what is being written about and what type of writing
- Knowing there is an audience for it can be intimidating
- Worrying that ideas will run out or come to nothing
- Finding it hard to relax when you're writing
- Getting lost in my writing – not knowing where I am or what's left to do
- Getting coherence, a coherent narrative

The positive side of emotions in writing

There are plenty of positive emotions associated with writing too.

Developing ideas and arguments or clarifying and organizing thoughts

A large number of students view the activity of writing very positively in terms of an aid to furthering, clarifying and organizing their own thinking:

- To develop your ideas fully and think it through

- Discovering new thoughts, or lines of argument
- To sort and categorize ideas and thoughts
- Putting ideas across coherently, in a structured way
- Making arguments more precise, and strong
- Writing helps to structure the thinking

Writing as part of learning and thinking

In a similar vein to the first, this second category of comments relates to students' views that writing can help them to learn, think and understand, for example:

- Clarification of thinking
- Learning or committing to memory through writing
- Achieving a higher level of understanding by writing
- Spotting the gaps in knowledge or in data
- Slowed pace of work, a more patient and measured approach

Catharsis, 'getting it out', making it tangible

Students express the idea or metaphor of a 'gap' between brain and paper, and closing that gap or making thoughts tangible:

- Writing is cathartic! Getting it out of your head
- Awareness, having to face up to things which are committed to paper
- A way of keeping hold of thoughts, and preserving them for later
- Once written you can examine and evaluate ideas

A source of reward and enjoyment

For a surprising number, writing is seen to have its own intrinsic rewards:

- A challenge and an opportunity
- Entertainment and enjoyment
- Feeling of being productive and creative is rewarding
- Good feedback is rewarding
- It builds confidence
- A way to tell a story and express a view

Reaching out and disseminating

Finally, several students see writing as a way of communicating, reaching a wider audience, connecting into their field and becoming 'part of the debate':

- Joining in the debate
- Marketing ideas, helping to reach out to others
- Telling a story
- Drawing attention to a particular field, theory, methodology
- Communicating with others
- Disseminating work

Several points emerge in reflecting on the affective domain. First, the affective domain in writing is extremely important to doctoral students who talk about it with enthusiasm and in depth. Second, they have many positive attitudes and feelings towards writing. These are well worth celebrating and building upon; what might you do to cultivate your positive feelings about writing. Third, the activity of opening up to think and talk about emotions in writing with fellow students is a vitally important one – not only to make you 'feel better' about writing but also as a starting point to help develop and improve your own relationships with writing. Fourth, negatively experienced feelings of stress, fear, isolation and anxiety are common. Such feelings of anxiety can paralyse progress and need to be acknowledged and managed. Finally, we hold and share with others the view that writing is a social practice (Aitchison and Lee 2006), and feelings about writing will be influenced by the behaviour and attitudes of others around you, and the perceived attitudes and behaviours of those unknown audiences who will read your writing. The activity of writing is likely to involve all these variables at one time or another. As Nightingale (1988, page 279) puts it, 'There is no such thing ... as writing skill which can be pasted like a veneer over all content in all contexts.' This personal context, your relationship to your data, to your research environment and to your writing, matters and is worth reflecting on.

Project manage your thesis

Your thesis, however much time you have until your deadline, is a large project which has to be delivered on a set date. If you are inclined to love following a process, you can borrow, adapt and apply the tools and ways of thinking from project management science to help you organize and plan your route through the project.

Outline the project brief

To make a start which takes you in the right direction, it's a good plan to know what you are aiming for and have an idea of what a 'good' doctoral thesis looks like. Having a project brief which defines the parameters of the product you aim to produce will help you know what you are aiming for. Doctorates are all unique, so you won't be able to find one which is just like yours, but you can get a broad idea from the students who have gone just before you in your discipline area. Use this and any previous writing you have already done towards your thesis to map out a detailed outline, get it down to roughly a sub-subheadings level of detail. Also check out the details of the expectations around a doctoral thesis in your university's Code of Practice for Research Degrees (your local version might be a variation on this title). Most Code of Practice type documents are available online, and set out any style, formatting, binding or submission process expectations for your institution (and you can also find out the process of submission, examination and completion in the same place). You could use these style guides to create template documents for your chapters and format as you write rather than leaving it all to the end.

Get your stakeholders on board

Take some time to map out who you will need to get on board with this writing project. Who will you need to involve and at which stages? These are your thesis stakeholders. You will obviously need your supervisor(s) to guide, provide feedback and eventually sign off on the thesis, but who else might you need? Is now the right time to discuss and informally arrange your thesis examiners? Check out the printers and binders you will need to use to have the physical document produced, what are their turnaround times? Do you need to agree copyright arrangements with publishers in order to include information or figures from your research papers in your thesis? What about colleagues who can proofread for you, are they primed and ready? And do friends, colleagues and family know that you are about to begin this project, is there any particular support you need from them?

Resource management and time budgets

What resources do you need to complete this project? Clearly Wi-Fi, tea and biscuits will need to be in plentiful supply, and what else? Your time is a resource and so is your supervisor's time, what are the time budgets you are working with? How many hours a week … or a day can you commit to this project? We know this will be less straightforward to answer, and more complicated to organize if you have family to care for, or job responsibilities in addition to your doctoral work. How many hours will you need to find to complete this project – this is a very hard one to estimate. Ever wondered how much you can write in an hour? Well why not experiment with what you can achieve in an hour, and use your findings to map out your time. One resource we all feel we can use more of is time, and we can fall into the trap of waiting for big chunks of free time to appear before we can get going on these projects. Look at your diary for the coming week though, where can you fit in a few thirty minutes or one hour of thesis-writing sessions across the next seven days? We strongly recommend that you factor in some time off from thesis writing too, and some time to reward yourself, however you decide, for reaching your milestones. You have a finite energy budget too, and so resting is a positive move towards completion.

Risk assessment

What are the costs and the benefits associated with thesis writing? This might sound redundant, if you don't write it, you won't get the doctorate. However this is a pertinent question to ask yourself if you are wondering if now is the right time for you to start. Perhaps you are weighing up the costs and benefits of collecting or analysing more data first *versus* starting your writing up now, which is a discussion we have often with the doctoral students we support. Perhaps you are wondering if you need to take a break to recharge your batteries before starting the writing project. Perhaps you are wondering if you should get a conference, grant proposal or job application out of the way first. Or possibly it's a family holiday, promotion at or exam period you are wondering if you should prioritize. Ask yourself: What do you risk or gain by starting now, what do you risk or gain by delaying? This decision will be personal to you in each case.

Milestones

Milestones mark specific points along the project timeline you have created. These points may signal anchors such as a project start and end date signed to the start and end points of different chapters or sections, or may flag a point at which you will need external review, feedback, input or checking. Milestones generally identify the major progress points that must be reached to achieve success. What are your milestones? How are you sectioning the project into manageable pieces? Don't forget to have a mini-celebration when each one is completed, keep up your momentum for starting the next one. You can even sneakily start on the next milestone before finishing the previous one, that way you don't lose momentum when you have to start from the blank page again.

Monitoring of project performance

Are you meeting or missing your milestone deadlines? Do you need to adjust your timings based on new data, or are you right on track? Have you perhaps budgeted too much time for the smaller pieces of work? In the next section we discuss more about how setting yourself up with an unrealistic plan can demotivate you. See the first couple of milestones as a test bed for planning the timeline of the rest.

Define the critical path

We don't recommend that you go away and read up on the complexities of critical path analysis algorithms, we don't want to provide you with distractions. In simple terms critical path analysis is looking logically at the thesis and deciding what order to do things in to maximize what can be done in the shortest space of time. It looks at which tasks are dependent on which other tasks, and it helps you prioritize what to do first. It prevents you from finding out later that you've got a delay in your progress because you did things in the wrong order. We are sure that you will always be able find something else to do in that downtime though.

Project logistics

Where are you physically going to do the writing? Will you work at home, in your department lab or office space, in the library, in a coffee shop, in a writing group, or will you vary it? Do you have access to those spaces at the times you will need them? What will you need with you in order to write? Is it all contained within your laptop, or will you need to carry physical papers around with you? How about security access, physically to buildings, or electronically to university networks and file stores? Have you got your VPN (virtual private network) set up? Is there confidentiality around any of your documents or data, which means you can't take them off site? Have you enough space in your cloud storage for large image or audio files? And finally, how will you gain access to research conversations and communities, to keep momentum up, and for fact checking of what you are writing? We recommend that if at all possible you spend at least some portion of your writing time in and around your department.

Quality assurance

To quality assure your thesis is to check that what you are producing is up to the standard expected for doctoral writing. Getting feedback from those around you, perhaps other doctoral students, writing groups, any postdocs you may have around, and your supervisor(s) is one way to do this. Another is to compare what you're writing back to those successful recent theses you sourced to plan yours.

Does 'something every day' work for you?

When Kay started the thesis mentoring programme, she used to be a big advocate of the mantra 'Write Something Every Day', which is a phrase often used in supporting writers, and is the essence of global academic writing initiatives. In using it, she always intended to recognize the need to begin to build habits and daily practices around writing. After all, doing something every day can only help it become second nature to you right? Practice makes perfect, doesn't it? And isn't genius equal to 1 per cent inspiration 99 per cent perspiration?

In reality, the way to build a habit that's useful and sustainable to you is somewhat more nuanced that simply 'do something every day'. What do you do every day? When do you do it? How is it done? And whom do you need to help you? In order to make these standard pieces of advice useable, we need to ground them in the reality that we are all different people, with busy lives and other commitments, and experiencing the range of human emotions that are common in achieving difficult tasks. We aren't robots, and planning to write every day isn't the same as actually writing every day.

What we think is very useful and helpful to thesis writers about the phrase 'something every day' is that it acknowledges the idea that thesis writing is a long-term project, that you need to pace yourself, and that you can iteratively and cumulatively build a thesis by doing a small amount and often. It helps to think that thesis writing can be done a bit at a time, and helps us take advantage of small opportunities for writing, and therefore avoid putting off starting until we get a full free day, week or month. There's good intention behind using the phrase in our support for thesis writers; we want to advise you to keep up momentum and enthusiasm for the task, make sure you're not consumed by it, and ultimately we want to help you to get it completed by your deadline, by breaking it down into small units which you can tackle piecemeal.

If your daily planner contains nothing else but writing, 'something every day' will be fairly achievable for you! However, where it can be unhelpful for us to say to ourselves 'I must write something every day' is if we know that, for us, it's just not going to be possible. If you are writing your thesis and working in a new role to pay the bills, finishing your data collection and analysis, working in your real-life day job, trying to get a journal article written, or creating slides for conferences, it will pay to think more realistically about where writing can manageably fit in and around these other priorities. Thesis writing can often slide to the bottom of a busy to-do list because firstly it's unfamiliar territory, there are more unknowns and so we perceive it as harder. And secondly There are fewer stakeholders in your thesis (often just you), and it can feel self-indulgent to write it at the expense of your colleagues, students or family.

If you plan to write every day for six months, and then on day three you don't manage it, how do you cope with that? Some of us will say 'OK, never mind, start again tomorrow'. Some of us will feel terribly guilty about it and chastize ourselves that we weren't able to follow the plan we spent time making. Creating a good plan that keeps up momentum and keeps you motivated stems from good awareness of what works for you, not from looking for the next easy win solution and creating rigid plans that set you up to fail. If you know from experience that you can't get writing done at home for example, or that you'll never write on Sundays, don't plan to. Why set yourself up to fail? It's very demotivating to miss goals and deadlines and it adds to feelings of panic and being overwhelmed. So what plan would be realistic for you?

EXERCISE: *Identify some blocks of time you could write over the next week, keep it little and often. At the end of each writing session, notice the time, place, the tasks you worked on and how you feel about them, and give yourself a mark out of five for productivity. Then look for opportunities the following week to do more of what works, and less of what doesn't.*

You can use this information to create a writing plan that sets a balance between acknowledging and managing your other work and home priorities, and pushing your thesis writing up the list as an important priority task managed over short stints.

CHAPTER FOUR

Writing and thinking as partner processes

Writing as a form of thinking

We've often come across a 'I have to complete my thinking before I can write' attitude to putting pen to paper. This resonates with the claim made some time ago by Torrance and Thomas (1994, 107) that many students seemed 'to see a strict demarcation between collecting data, or doing research, and the writing up of this material as a thesis'. Quite rightly, Torrance and Thomas add that 'this perception may itself be a cause of problems'. Holding this assumption creates anxiety, fear and tension, with the outcome for many being total paralysis in writing.

The view that ideas must be conceived and fully shaped before the writing process can begin is a general problem in writing which Torrance et al. comment on, as do several others (such as Elbow 1973 and Bazerman 1983). It has been labelled the 'knowledge telling' model (Bereiter and Scardamalia 1987) in the sense that writing is seen as a simple transfer of ready-conceived ideas from brain to paper or screen. We have met students who do not see their writing in this way – they talk of using writing to organize, shape and crystallize their ideas for example (see Chapter 3). Yet surprisingly, many we encounter do still speak of being in the 'writing up' phase, and universities sometimes still refer to the 'writing-up year' of a doctorate. We would like to promote and encourage you to view writing as part of the thinking process, that is, that writing should be seen as 'knowledge developing' rather than knowledge telling. We suggest that your writing should start as soon as possible, become a habit of practice, and be used as a tool to develop thinking and understanding – as opposed to a process which simply transfers thoughts from brain to paper, that is, a mental state to a physical one. (One excellent writer on this view is Laurel Richardson, who talks of writing being a method of inquiry: 1998). As Torrance and Taylor (1994,109) put it, 'The process of writing is integral to the research process as a whole.'

Crafting a writing plan you can stick to

Most institutions, or supervisors, will ask you to complete a thesis plan at some stage in the doctoral study period. Each institution, or research group, may provide its own guidance on the thesis plan formally as part of a student handbook or workshop, or informally as shared tips and ways of working passed down from student to student. Thesis plans can range in their requirements from a simple overview of the content of the thesis chapters, to an in-detail skeleton of the thesis content containing sections and subsections, to a full project plan that asks students to timeline the writing process and factor in time for feedback, revision and formatting.

As with all planning and scoping activities, the plan that works for you is going to be the one you can stick to. We are not going to prescribe how you should plan your time and budget your energy, but we will, in the coaching spirit, give you a few pitfall factors to think about to help you create something that works for you and that you can use to guide yourself and to track and review the writing process. These pointers are derived from our many discussions and coaching sessions with thesis writers who each had their own individual approach to getting to the end and submitting their completed thesis.

Every week I make a plan for writing but I ignore it and end up with no progress.

Things that might stop you from creating thesis writing plan that works in practice:

Being in denial about the thesis

Whether you think about it or you don't, your thesis does need writing, and it needs you to write it. Whether or not you plan it, you will still have to write it to be awarded the doctorate. Whether you start now or start later, you will still have to write it if you want to finish the degree. Having to author a large document, a book in fact, which justifies everything you've been doing for the last few years can understandably evoke feelings of anxiousness and make you fearful. After all it's something you've not done before, and likely don't know how to do at the beginning. Your examiners will be judging you on this, it's important, and so your feelings of apprehension are valid. Avoiding making a plan is a way to keep the fear of judgement at a distance. Subconsciously we feel we can avoid the vulnerability involved in sharing our work for critique if we just don't start. But logically, this isn't going to work. You still need to write the thesis.

Not knowing really what a thesis should look or read like or what the requirements are, and having little contact time from my supervisors to get feedback, is making me overly stressed.

You don't like planning

Some of us are not natural planners, we just like to get started on a task and see what happens. Minimal planning is a valid way of working, and this approach has some clear advantages in that it can be more responsive and flexible. The difficulty is though that we're often writing a thesis in a fairly fixed format and towards a deadline, and it helps you to know if you'll meet that deadline if you can monitor and track your progress throughout. This helps you feel more secure about the process, and it also gives you a chance to celebrate the small goals as well as the big ones. Additionally, we know that the tasks that we take time to visualize, describe, sort and order are more likely to get done simply because the way forward is presented as a clear set of steps and stages. If you just need to get it done, take yourself out for a treat, get comfy, and get it started.

I'm not very good at working on something gradually over time – I have always done last-minute bursts of work or all-nighters, but recently the pieces of work have been too long for this approach to work, and so I come away failing and feeling like the task is insurmountable.

The goal isn't clear – what and by when?

It's always a good idea to know what you need to achieve and the time frame for delivery. A good first starting point is to confirm when your final thesis submission deadline is. Perhaps you can do this by checking your online student record, making a phone call to the right team in student services, or talking to your department's administrator in charge of doctoral students. Does your university have policies on completion times that you need to be aware of? Does your department have local regulations and milestones it expects you to achieve so you can demonstrate you're making progress? Does your supervisor expect the thesis to be written to a particular timeline? It's worth a discussion. The next step is to get a good understanding of what you need to produce on that timeline, take a look at some good examples of doctoral theses from your discipline area, and note down the structure, sections, style, level of detail etc. What does a good thesis look like? Compare two or three and note – Are they of a similar formula? Are there differences in the structure, tone, emphasis, proportions? As you go, map it to your thesis – What will you need to include, what is similar to and what is different from your research?

All aims and no objectives

The thesis is a large document of many parts, and writing it comprises several stages of varying critical depth, and many individual tasks, and writing processes (e.g. drafting, redrafting, feedback, refining). Saying to yourself 'today I'm going to write my thesis' is a fine inspirational mantra, but it doesn't describe what you're going to do in any level of detail. It's all aims (the end goal), and no objectives (the task list). Murray and Moore (2006) have written in detail on how setting specific and small objectives, or 'prompts', for writing can help academic writers to maximize their productivity, and make every spare 30-minute writing session count. The idea is to decide for each of your writing sessions what you can achieve in that amount of time, and to write yourself an objective to work to. So for example instead of saying to yourself 'I'm going to write Chapter 3 for 90 minutes', you might write yourself a specific objective something like 'In this 90-minute session I am going to draft a three paragraphs introducing my data, I will need to cover [point 1], [point 2], and [point 3]'.

To get things done, I need to create a very detailed thesis plan rather than focusing on just writing stuff as and when. This allows me to see what is likely to be in each chapter, what my arguments will say and what evidence I need for them.

It needs fresh eyes on it – you need your plan validated

Perhaps you've started making a plan, and you're feeling stuck. Have you produced the right thing? Does it cover everything? Are you wondering if it's a comprehensive outline? Does it contain everything it needs to? Does it have too much in the literature review? Does your plan present your data in the right way? It's time to show the plan to someone else and get their feedback. A supervisor is ideal as they will be tuned into how your research fits in with the wider research field. As a pre-check though, you could find an ally in your department, perhaps another student, a research associate, or another staff member who can spare you a few minutes. Getting fresh eyes on a problem can help you spot gaps, and talking to more people can help you identify new developments in the field you may have missed. Don't forget though that you have final say over what's in and what's out.

I am a capable writer but have had huge trouble identifying how to structure an argument for a thesis. I do now really need to get this plan to my supervisors, who know what a good thesis looks like and can tell me if I'm hitting the mark.

There isn't a right place to start

People often ask us the right place to start with thesis writing, wondering what chapter they should write first. I can never answer that question for you because there is no one single right place for everyone to start. Some of you will be 'best bits first' people, who will want to start with the parts of the thesis that are more descriptive and gain writing experience and confidence to spur you on to the more intellectually involved content. Some of you will be 'worst bits first' people, who want to get the sections or tasks you find harder or less enjoyable out of the way first, clearing a path to the finish line. Neither is right or wrong: approach it in a way that will be helpful to you. The key is to just start somewhere (you can always change your mind!) and remove the block of thinking that there's a best place to start. If you're really stuck for a way into thesis writing, then revisit writing and resources you already have. Do you have a report prepared from your confirmation review you can revisit and adapt? Do you have data figures you have prepared that you can write descriptions of? Do you have journal articles you've read which are covered in notes you could type up into draft material?

I am failing to put pen to paper. I seem to be scared of committing to finalizing my thoughts and opinions on things.

What got you here won't get you there

You will have a lot of past work and study experience you can draw on to help you plan and manage your thesis writing project. Be prepared to learn some new ways of getting writing work done too, you don't need to know it all before you start. To borrow from Goldsmith and Reiter (2008), 'what got you here' – the methods and study processes that you used to attain the qualifications and academic level you have completed previously – may not necessarily be all you need 'to get you there', to the end of the thesis writing process. That's not to say you're doing it wrong; you aren't, it is just that you can expect to develop a new set of complementary writing habits and thought processes which will work with the academic abilities you already have. As an example, to a greater or lesser extent depending on your prior experiences, the criticality needed for this type of writing may be new to you, and you may expect that discussing your data in the context of the existing literature is something you will have to learn how to do as you go.

I'm starting to realize that a lack of deadlines is an absolute killer for writing productivity; it's a major change from undergraduate and master's study, and wasn't really noticed in the first two years of my PhD as experimental work at the bench necessitated sticking to a tight schedule and guidelines, and was thus easy to stay motivated for. It's harder to have a beginning and end for a day when writing now.

What worked for them, won't work for you

In group discussions with thesis writers, we will ask people to share the tips and techniques for thesis writing that they've found useful. Inevitably a thesis writer enthused by having found a good way to motivate themselves will eagerly share the tip, for example, 'I just work in 25-minute bursts and then take a break' only to be met with someone else saying 'No! I tried that and it didn't work at all'. Clearly it's not a bad tip because the person who shared it is using it to great effect, but we can't expect all ways of increasing our productivity to work for all people. If we could simply prescribe a writing template, a method and a timetable for you, things would be very easy, and there would be no need for the many books on thesis writing there are available. The key is to notice what works for you. You can do this by noticing where, when and how you do your best work and then simply doing more of what works for you, and less of what doesn't work. Yes it's good to know your options, what's out there for you to try, but we advise against spending all your time reading books, blogs and articles trying to find the best way to write. Listen to yourself, you know what's best for you.

You're lured and soothed by the academic comfort zone

Doesn't it always feel like there are so many things popping up that need your immediate attention and take the focus away from writing the thesis? Perhaps it's a deadline for a conference abstract, a research group meeting or seminar talk you've been signed up for? A class you're teaching next week? Maybe it's an article you're writing with other people that needs your attention and input ASAP? Or it is data collection and analysis: Do you just need to do one more interview or experiment to complete the set? When we talk about procrastination in thesis writing, we often think of desk-tidying or tea-making behaviour – the obvious things that help us avoid getting on with the big important task we need to face up to. Do check though that you're not using things that are legitimate and important pieces of academic work to avoid the thesis. Be aware of your academic comfort zone – the things you are confident doing and that make you feel like you've achieved something – it can suck you in. We're certainly not telling you to dump the teaching work and the conferences etc., these are important in career building too. Instead we are advocating that you strike balance between all these other tasks and finishing your thesis, finding some time each week to get some thesis writing done. It's a case of finding compromises for the other tasks, deciding what's for now, and what's for later. What opportunities are you prepared to miss this year, or this semester? What can wait until you've secured your doctorate? What analysis is essential and what is only nice to have? You can always come back to data collection and analysis once you've got a chunk of writing done.

Procrastination is a time sink. I'm even procrastinating academically by convincing myself it's a good idea to spend time research this exciting new area that is completely unrelated to anything in my thesis, instead of just doing the work that needs to be done.

You don't know how long each thing takes

If your thesis master plan signs you up to unwittingly unrealistic daily writing targets, and unachievable goals, it won't take long to demotivate yourself. I've met with a good few people who aimed to finish the thesis entirely in twelve weeks only to then realize that this won't be possible as things like eating and sleeping are getting in the way. They get very demotivated by setting themselves up to fail and frustrated that they can't give all their energy to thesis writing. Sense check the plan you are making for yourself: Does it look manageable or are you going to get off track within the first week? Often people will overestimate how much they can achieve in an hour, a day or a week, and when the inevitable happens, they get demotivated. The good news is that you're researchers! Why not try having a week or two collecting data about how fast you write, what you can achieve in a 2-hour burst, and how long you can sustain writing before you get fatigued? You can use this new information then to create a writing plan for the next couple of weeks that's tailored to you.

I log the actual time I use every day, so I can clearly see how many hours I spent on this chapter or that chapter, or reading academic journals etc. This is very helpful as I can get to know my productivity, and how many hours I need to plan for various parts. As the PhD progresses it's ok to make changes to your working patterns to reflect these fluctuations, rather than maintaining a regimented routine at all times.

You're expecting someone else to keep track for you

In order to know if you're on track to meet your plan, you have to actively keep track and monitor your progress. Adding up your total word count could do this (always recognizing that this will fluctuate as you refine and edit texts). Or perhaps you are ticking off the subsections of your thesis plan as you go. A rough percentage calculation will help you check in on your plan and know if you're on target to reaching your deadline. At the half way point, are you half way there? I advise you to manage this process for yourself, don't wait to be told that's enough now and you can move on to the next section.

You're replicating mistakes or steering off course

Getting 'early and often' feedback on your progress is the way to sense check what you are producing as you go. It will help you avoid making the same sorts of errors multiple times throughout all your writing, or getting off course by perhaps over-expanding a section or spending too long perfecting one area of the thesis to the detriment of later sections. Writing your thesis is a learning process.

You get better at it as you go along because you learn how to do it by actually doing it. A writing plan that factors in some points at which you stop for a while to think things through and check in with others can help you consolidate what you have learnt from writing the previous section, and adjust your plan going forward. Getting an external eye on your work, or talking it through with someone, means that anything you've assumed, missed or misunderstood can be addressed before too much work is done and needs to be redone. This feedback doesn't necessarily have to be formal supervisor to student written feedback. Asking a colleague to cast an eye over your writing, perhaps in a reciprocal arrangement, can be really helpful in spotting the obvious mistakes, typos, commas, grammar and wrong references. Reading others' works in progress too can be reassuring as you see their thought processes, and new ideas can spark from sharing and discussing work in this way. You will benefit from, and you are entitled to, some formal feedback on your work from supervisors too. To get this feedback you are going to have to show them the work you've done. We know it can be quite hard to give work over for comment and critique; feeling safe to do this requires a certain amount of trust to be present in the supervision relationship. Remember that the doctorate, as well as the writing process, is a learning experience; you can expect that your writing won't begin and end with the first attempt. Even very experienced academic writers will draft and redraft work, so getting input from an experienced writer is a normal and expected part of the process.

You're striving for perfect first time

The term 'perfectionist' is mooted about in research institutions, sometimes as an aspirational personal value, or a self-deprecating academic inevitability. But perfectionism can actually be fairly crippling in terms of being able to achieve writing productivity. That's because perfection is not only a subjective but also a needlessly severe standard to aim for, and refusing to accept any standard short of perfection means your goal is always unattainable. Accuracy is clearly very important when you're breaking new ground, and contributing new knowledge as you will be in your doctorate. Suggesting new theories and mechanisms from your research data is clearly not something you want to approach in a sloppy way;

after all this is the document you will be examined on and which your examiners will use to decide if you've reached doctorateness or not. Bear in mind though that 'perfectionism' is not equal to being 'precise', or 'accurate'. An accurate, precise, well-written text in the appropriate style, and aligned with the conventions and discourses of your research area, is achievable. But don't feel you have to get it right first time – academic writing is a process of drafting and redrafting. Ask the academic writers around you how many iterations their last research paper went through. How many versions did they create in revising their most recent grant proposal? We bet it's more than one! It's a rare person who can sit down and write a coherent story straight out of their brain. Most of us have to pour out our thoughts and fragments of thoughts and half-baked ideas onto paper, and then start sorting them into a linear story. The brain can connect thoughts to ideas and to data in a huge networked map of messiness. To make sense of the mess and order it into a critical reasoned argument, you need to tip out what's in your brain and start the refinement process. If you wait until your idea is perfect in your head, then you will never write it.

I went from the crippling thinking that I had to pour a perfect version out of my head, to recognizing the need to read, reread, write, rewrite, think, rethink, understand, re-understand. This is normal process, not me being thick!

You didn't factor in negotiating the time of other people you need

Let's imagine you have diligently crafted a plan with everything nicely broken down into sections and subsections, with feedback time factored in at regular intervals and time to adapt and amend your work based on the comments from your supervisors. Don't forget the crucial aspect of communicating that plan and flexing it to get agreement with the people you are going to need to help you. Although you are entitled to expect some writing feedback and guidance from your supervisor, exactly how, when and in what way it should be done must be decided by a process of negotiation with your supervisor or supervision team. Remember this matters most to you, and so you will naturally be very focused on getting it done as a priority. For your supervisor, and rightly so, it will not be the most important piece of work on their to-do list. They will have other teaching and research work to manage, other student queries and correspondence to deal with, they'll be thinking about the papers they are writing and the funding they are applying for and probably a hundred other things. Commonly they will thank you to own and manage this process and agree their part with you. Ask them what is reasonable for them as a timeline? When are the good and bad times to be seeking feedback? When are they (and you) going to be away from the department and out of communication? How long will they need to read three pages, and how long for thirty pages? How many pages at a time do they want to see ideally? And how would they prefer to give feedback? Do they like to write it or is it easier for them to talk face-to-face or via Skype? When you're working with multiple supervisors you will need to double that negotiation – Which supervisor will feedback on which sections? Do all supervisors need to see all parts of the thesis and all draft versions? Who wants to see the work first and who second? Try to view the agreement you make as a formal agreement and we advise you to do your best to keep to it. Keep in touch if you're going to miss a deadline, don't let it sail by and then expect that everyone's timelines will adjust to accommodate you.

You didn't factor in the 'hidden work' of writing

A good proportion of the preparation of the thesis is about writing administration and writing management. It's romantic to think of thesis writing in terms of the more creative aspects where you might imagine yourself typing in free-flow, creating conclusive arguments that put forth your world-changing, groundbreaking ideas. When you imagine yourself thesis writing, do you ever think about managing the integrity of redrafted content by using version control, clear labelling or tracked changes? Are you imagining yourself keeping track of your referencing and checking the fine details in your reference manager? There will be thesis formatting to do, for example, getting the layouts on large documents right, page numbering, creating a table of contents, a table of figures and a table of tables. What about the formal permissions you'll need if you want to use other images in your thesis that you haven't personally created? If you've published from your doctorate, and the content of the article(s) will be used in your thesis, it's likely you'll have some negotiating to do with the publisher to gain permission to include the content. Getting in touch early will mean you're not delayed in the final stages by someone else's out-of-office email reply exactly when you need help. And don't forget that it's likely you'll need to print it out and get the document bound into a volume for submission. How long does this usually take at your university binders? When are their busy periods? Have you got enough paper and access to a decent printer? We say this not to add stress to your thesis writing, but so you can prepare in advance to tie up all the loose ends and permissions, and spare yourself from last-minute panic. These are all things that we have seen cause unnecessary stress and delay in preparing the thesis.

I had to learn to implement a more strategic set up for myself. I used to work as hard as possible and as long as possible, but in the long run it's not good for me to work like that.

Finding buddies, mentors, groups and communities

In Chapter 1 we have covered the importance of staying connected. But what if you don't have easy access to an established thesis mentoring programme? How do you access these types of conversations? Let's look at some ways in which you can get similar benefits:

How to make good use of a writing buddy?

A writing buddy is a colleague or friend with whom you check in regularly, either face-to-face or online. The focus of the check-ins can be whatever works for you both. You may want to just meet for a coffee and talk it over informally. Or for a more focused conversation: you could keep each other motivated by declaring your word count each week by email, you could review your progress and set targets together for the coming weeks, or you may want to swap drafted work and proofread for each other before sending it to your supervisors. If there's not an obvious buddy available, you could email around your department and see if anyone picks up, or stick up a poster; try asking your supervisor, PGR administrator, or Researcher Training and Development colleagues if they know of anyone else looking for, or who would benefit from, a writing buddy.

> *I was at a low ebb, when I had no one to talk to. Someone non-judgemental, who can understand the difficulties, if only to have a gripe at, it's reassuring. Sure they can offer you advice on practicalities, but in a psychological sense it's just reassuring.*

How to find and recruit a thesis mentor

An advantage of working with a thesis mentor is that you don't have to reciprocate and mentor them too. A thesis mentor is any neutral third party who is prepared to spend some focused time with you, helping to unpick how you are doing, where you are stuck and how to move forward again. You bring the coffee, they bring the cheerleading. There are pay-for mentoring and coaching services you can find by Internet searches, but in our opinion, a good choice for a thesis mentor is a postdoctoral researcher, not too close to your research area. Choosing someone who is a step removed from your field helps you resist the temptation to talk about your research project, rather than your writing progress. Having support for both project work (supervisor) and writing (mentor) creates a complementary approach. Many postdocs are interested in teaching and will need to evidence supervision, and teaching experience on their CVs, or in professional accreditation applications, so this has benefits for the mentor too. Again, if there's no obvious mentor in your direct vicinity, try getting a recommendation from your PGR administrator, or Researcher Training and Development colleagues, who know a lot of research staff. Once you have identified a potential mentor, write to them and let them know exactly what you are looking for, what you'd need from them and why you have chosen them. An email text you could adapt is below:

Dear [mentor of choice],

My name is [name], I am a student with [supervisor] and I am writing my thesis currently; my deadline is [deadline].

Our colleague [name] has suggested you as/I thought you might be a person who would be good at, and could be interested in, doing some 'thesis mentoring' work with me over the next few weeks. I thought I'd approach you to see if you are interested and tell you a bit more about what I am looking for.

I foresee mentoring being for about an hour every fortnight, and giving me the benefits of checking in on my progress, and setting some targets for my writing. I am not looking for any special advice, or for you to know all the answers, or for a replacement supervisor. I would like a mentor who simply listens to me talk through what I am planning to do, and helps me put together a plan of action that works for me. And of course sharing any tips you have would be welcome. I would not expect you to proofread my work, or guide me on the content of the thesis.

What do you think? Could we meet/chat on the phone/Skype and see if this is something that we'd like to do?

With thanks

[student]

Once you have recruited a person to be your mentor, some essential things to talk over and agree in your first meeting are:

- What is the focus of the sessions? That is, what are your main objectives for writing?

- How long will the mentoring last? A trial period? Followed by how many mentoring sessions?

- Confidentiality? Do you expect the mentor to keep what you tell them confidential?

- Responsibility. Who is responsible for keeping in touch, booking in the next meeting, and managing the partnership? We strongly suggest that you as the mentee should take on this responsibility.

And remember, a good mentor will minimize the advising they do, and instead focus on listening, asking you questions that encourage you to evaluate your situation. They will also encourage and support you to plan your own best way forward, not theirs.

I valued having someone to reflect with who has no immediate attachment to my success – an impartial ear who is able to make suggestions from a viewpoint that is unrelated.

How to start a writing group

A writing group is for you if you would like to focus on the processes of how writing is developed and gain input from other people. In a group, you can discuss writing, share your work in draft, get feedback on what you are producing and plan how to develop pieces further. The writing itself is done before or after the group sessions, and meeting regularly over several weeks or months allows to take work from conception to completion. It will also give you the opportunity to read what others write and compare your styles and approaches. You don't need a lot of people to have a good writing group, in fact a tight group of five or six is far more manageable than twenty. Skype works well for this type of group, so don't be put off if you're not on campus often. You will benefit more from the group if you commit to attending regularly, even if you feel you have not made enough progress, or feel what you produce is not ready to be seen, you will always get something positive out of it. A small group of thesis writers from your department would be ideal, but recruiting postdoctoral researchers writing papers, grants, fellowships etc. will achieve the same outcomes. Try meeting up monthly for four months and see how it goes. Each time you bring your current work in progress, swap and get feedback, and each time leave with an action plan to improve your writing. The action plan is important, so don't be tempted to skip it. Defining exactly what you need to do means you are more likely to go away and do it.

I reached out to a few people that I trust and now have a network of friends who I meet with regularly. That has completely changed my whole perspective of the PhD, and my outlook is so much more positive now that I don't feel alone.

How to run a writing retreat?

Structured Writing Retreats are spaces for people who want to get away from regular work or life, to focus on their writing. Retreats for academic writing purposes (Murray and Newton 2009) are now really popular in many institutions, and have been adapted from the original model in different ways to suit different schedules and locations. In brief, people come together in the same place at the same time and write in silence – the writing is done within the group sessions. They start and stop writing at the same time, and take breaks together. This, as well as offering protected time and space to get away from distractions, conveys some nice advantages over writing alone. The peer pressure of writing together (and making sure breaks are taken) removes the temptation to do other work or procrastinate on the Internet. The group dynamic also means that there is someone else with whom to set yourself some writing targets before starting. In contrast to a writing group, these sessions can be attended as and when you like, and the writing you produce is private to you. You don't need any specialist resources to set up a retreat. All you need to do is book a room for a day, or even a half day (think about power sockets!), and get a few friends together. Breaks are an integral part, so don't be tempted to miss them out, and you can add writing warm-ups and goal-setting conversations or simply just get on and write. You may want to link your retreat to the Shut Up and Write movement and just do short 30 minutes – 1 hour sessions together followed by coffee break.

Social media

Let's say it upfront and clearly, do not get too distracted by social media! We are not recommending you go away and read every single one of the resources below, procrastinate on Twitter, or spend hours looking for the golden tip that will make thesis writing easy. All this will do is make you waste your time and delay the inevitable point where you just have to get on with it. However, as aids to understanding your reactions to doctoral writing, reading about others' experiences can be useful. And as outlets for your frustrations, and as ways to get your questions answered, social media can serve you pretty well.

Blogs

There are a good number of blogs about academic writing and the doctoral experience, producing a very credible commentary on the current landscape of research. Our current favourites are listed in the further reading section and are worth keeping an eye on. There are also tens to hundreds of blogs written by doctoral students about their subject area, or about the PhD experience, or both. We have not listed them all here, but a quick Google search will give you a lot of hits to investigate and choose from. What about having a go at writing a blog yourself? Blogging your own ideas about research (do take care though not to disclose your unpublished data) and thesis writing, in plain language not bogged down by referencing, can help you to figure out what you want to say about your work, and it can also help you work through your approach to getting your thesis written. In essence it's like a public (should you choose to make it so) diary or daily journal. Others may find it helpful to read too, but more importantly you may find it helpful to get the thoughts out of your head and into another space. There are a number of free blogging platforms and tools, and blogs are now so easy to get started you can have one up and running within the hour. Maybe now is not the time to get distracted by writing a blog if you should be writing a thesis, but if you find it useful, you could try keeping posts short and using blogging to chart your thesis progress. And of course there's no requirement to publish your writing diaries to feel the benefit, you can keep them to yourself.

Twitter

You can get some of the benefit of Twitter without even making an account; tweets are in general publicly available and there are plenty of accounts out there signposting to articles and resources for doctoral students and covering broad topics such as methodologies, professional development, writing and careers. Twitter helps you find things out anonymously and follow up leads without anyone knowing you were there. To be able to post anything, you will need to make yourself an account. Again this can be done anonymously, simply choose a pseudonym and a photo of an Internet cat and off you go. To get the full benefit of Twitter though, it's worth engaging as yourself and joining in the global conversations with others (Mewburn and Thompson 2013) as a real person. Twitter can help you access the opinions of a wide community of researchers across lots of locations. You can test ideas out in the communities you join or build, and you can ask for help, support, ideas, answers and resources – and give back these things too. Twitter can be used to find allies and build informal learning groups and social networks, making visible the processes of research, not just the products (McPherson et al. 2010). Or it can be used simply to remind you that you aren't alone in striving to finish your doctorate. Ready to get started? Try searching for tweets that contain the hashtags #PhD, #thesis, #PhDhelp, #phdchat, #phdadvice, #PhDProblems, #PhDlife, #shouldbewriting, #shutupandwrite, #AcWri (Academic Writing) and #AcaDowntime.

- PhD2Published: Frost, C., Tarrant, A. http://www. phd2published.com

- Explorations of Style: Cayley, R. https://explorationsofstyle. com

- Thesis Whisperer: Mewburn, I. https://thesiswhisperer.com

- Doctoral Writing SIG: Aitchison, C., Guerin, C., Carter, S., https://doctoralwriting.wordpress.com

- Patter: Thomson, P., https://patthomson.net

CHAPTER FIVE

Reading and writing as joint functions

Any postgraduate study requires that you explore what is already 'known' in your area of research, what's been done before and, just as important, how it's been done. This is an aspect of research which many of us, including physical scientists at times, are apt to neglect. The main general rule is that any study should be located in the context of what has been done before. Your job is not just to mould your own brick but to slot it into the wall of existing understanding in that field.

Knowing where and when to stop reading is a far more difficult problem than knowing where to start. In some fields it is best to start from a seminal or much-cited paper and go from there – a method which can be called 'snowball searching' (c.f. snowball sampling). Each paper will have references at the end, which will lead to other references and so on. The problem is that the process is rather like a chain reaction, and the list of publications one 'should' read grows exponentially. The growth is multiplied when one begins to use the wide range of bibliographies, databases, indexes, lists and other sources which are available freely and electronically.

It is a lengthy business, but you have to stop at some time. Our main message in this chapter is that keeping an eye open for, seeking and reviewing literatures is an activity that should go on right up to the day of submitting your thesis.

Why review the literature?

The literature review can be seen as fulfilling a range of purposes: to engage with published work so that you can show how your study could add something; to provide a context and a conceptual or theoretical framework for your own research; sometimes, perhaps, to show a need for your own work; or most importantly, to show how your investigation relates to, and builds on, previous research. On a more cynical note, it may be used to show the examiners (for a thesis) or the reviewers (for an article) that you have 'done the reading'. However, its main purpose is to ensure that it builds on the work of others.

On a practical level, reviewing the literature is integral to thinking about the research that one is undertaking. It relates to the formulating of research questions, the framing and design of a study, the methodology and methods, the data analysis, and the final conclusions and recommendations. Undertaking a review of the literature allows any researcher to:

- Define what the field of study is, by identifying the theories, concepts, research and ideas with which the study connects

- Provide a historical and geographical context

- Establish what research has been already been done, which relates to the research question or field of study

- Identify and discuss methods and approaches which have been used by other researchers

- Identify the 'gaps' or further contribution which the present piece of research will make (note that the metaphor of a 'gap' can be a risky one)

The process of reviewing the literature encourages you to reflect on, and show, where your ideas have come from (Ridley 2012). For, as Murray (2002) points out, researchers are unlikely to have come up with something that is entirely new. The danger of claiming 'newness' or the presence of a 'gap' is that in practice it may just be that we have not yet found out what has already been done on this topic. Referring to and discussing existing literature will enable you to make realistic, substantiated claims about your area of study, and to avoid sweeping generalizations, by rooting the claims you make for your own research in the context of other studies and previous research.

The literature review process

The focus for a research study may come out of reading the work of other researchers: in that case the literature base should be clear. However, the focus for a study may come from an area of personal or professional interest, or it may be an area in which research has been encouraged by a supervisor or sponsoring organization, and is therefore at one step removed from the research literature.

As a researcher you need to read widely, but, equally, to avoid drowning in a sea of literature, you also need to read with your own study and its research questions in mind, thinking about how the literature you read relates to your own research. However, this implies that the focus of your study is clear before starting to explore the literature. In reality, both the focus and the research questions are likely to be developed and refined as a result of wider reading, and the question of 'where to start?' is a major challenge. One way of visualizing the range of literature you explore is to see it (as in Figure 3.1 later) as comprising literature at three levels: first, background material which is of broad relevance to your study; second, literature and research studies which address issues which are closely related to your study, or a part of your study; and finally, literature which is directly related to your study (Rudestam and Newton 1992).

Questions to ask not only at the early stage but also before you finally submit should include:

- What is known about the broad topic I am researching, and from what types of literature?

- What are the most important 'landmark' works within the field, referred to regularly in other studies?

- What methods and methodologies are being used to research the area I am interested in?

- What theoretical and conceptual frameworks are being used to understand the field?

Reading at this stage needs to be undertaken with an open mind, with a view to clarifying the focus of study, the methodological approach to be taken and the conceptual framework to be used. On the basis of wider reading, the following question can then be considered: Which areas of this work are centrally relevant to my topic and research questions?

Until you have undertaken initial wider reading, it is often difficult to address this question.

The big search: Computers and people

We do not have the space here to give detail on searching strategies. Many searching approaches take full advantage of the resources available through the World Wide Web – a comprehensive guide to searching and taking advantage of the Internet is provided by Hart (2001) and Ridley (2012).

Equally, other people's references are an obvious but sometimes overlooked source. Not only do references in books and journal papers direct you to further references, but they help you to develop a picture of what work is being cited regularly, and what work is informing the field – who is reading whom. This involves an iterative process of discovering regular reference to particular writers, reports and studies: a process that should carry on right up to the day of submission.

Opportunistic searching, such as browsing library shelves, looking through the contents lists of edited collections, looking at contents lists in journals, asking other people, and noting references to other work made at conferences and seminars, helps make connections and provides openings into relevant literature which no amount of detailed database searching will uncover.

One other valuable source is people. Researchers at all levels can sometimes use people who may be experts in the field. If you cannot arrange to see them, write, telephone or email them, asking for help and advice. It is surprising how many experts in a field are willing to give up time and energy to someone who is, or will be, working in the same field.

Last but not the least, libraries and subject librarians are important sources of ideas and help with searching for literature.

Our own experience of librarians is that they are invariably helpful and informative – quite simply, involving them will add value to your search.

Ultimately though, only you (the researcher) can decide which references to follow up, which ones to skim or which to examine closely, and which publications to 'weave into' the eventual thesis, report, article or book. The searching process has to stop somewhere. But the lines and boundaries can only be drawn by the researcher, and the drawing of these lines has to be justified in writing up.

What to collect, how to read and how to store it

Different types of literature review are discussed by Hammond and Wellington (2012, 99–102). For example, a 'systematic review' is a term used for a particular type of literature review which aims to give an overview or meta-analysis of primary studies which claim to have used explicit and reproducible methods. The term is commonly used to refer to reviews which debate and synthesize the findings of a number of research trials, often of a statistical nature. Although such reviews have tended to be more typical of medical and scientific research, they are now occurring more frequently in social science research.

However you go about reviewing the literature, you should be systematic in collecting, recording and organizing the literature. It is helpful to work out a strategy that works for you. Start with references and abstracts, and then decide which work you need to read in full. You are likely to want to revisit reading that you do early on, and you may well have a different interpretation of your reading once you have read more widely. Read enough of a book, but do not feel that you have to read it from cover to cover with the same attention to detail throughout.

It is vital to make a short summary of key points and comments on the overall arguments and thesis, in *your own words*, after reading. One of our doctoral students once said in a tutorial: 'Whenever I read something, I try to write something'. This is excellent advice for researchers at all levels.

Storing information, notes and references

Whether writing a book such as this, an article or a thesis, your life will be made a lot easier if you start saving your references right from the start, keeping all necessary details by following a recognized referencing system such as Harvard. There are several computer programmes specifically for this purpose such as EndNote (http://www.adeptscience.co.uk/products/refman/endnote/).

EndNote also allows you to make and store notes on your reading, which are attached to the relevant reference. However, a word processing programme also works for this purpose. A document containing all references encountered, which is regularly updated, can act as a source document for referencing all your writing. It is easier to select from references you have stored, than to hunt out full references at a later stage.

You will also want a system for storing papers, documents and notes. This needs to be a system that works for you, and allows you to find and use your reading in an effective way. You might therefore store material according to relevant themes in your work and then reorganize your collection of material as your work progresses. This can provide a visible, tangible way of making connections between different literatures and connecting, for example, policy and source documents with theoretical debates and concepts. (Ridley 2012, 79–97, gives useful, practical details on the important business of managing, organizing and storing references)

When to stop

Rather than seeing the literature review as a linear process, which has a start and an end, it is helpful to view collecting, reading, reviewing and writing about the literature as a cyclical process which ends only when you submit your thesis. Reading widely helps to clarify the research focus and research questions, but this is the first stage in the reviewing process, rather than the end of it. Revisiting and clarifying your research focus and questions allow you to refine your literature search and collection, to identify what literature you need to explore in more depth, and what 'gaps' there are in the literature you have explored to date. Repeating this process of returning to your research focus and clarifying it as a result of wider reading also helps to answer the question many students and researchers ask: 'How much literature is enough?' If your overall aim is to consider the theories, research, and ideas with which your study connects, then by returning to the aims and purposes of your study regularly, you should be able to clarify whether you have considered the range of literature which is relevant to your focus, and whether all the literature you have gathered is still relevant to your focus. So ... when to stop? The day you submit.

Writing while you read and reading while you write

All researchers face the danger of being overwhelmed by the sheer volume of literature that they feel that perhaps they should read. One source of comfort is to remind yourself that you cannot read everything (although one must read something!). Another strategy is to write while you read.

Thus the cyclical process mentioned above also applies to writing about the literature. Writing as you go along offers a way of creating a dialogue, which can be between you and your reading, between you and your supervisor, or between you and other researchers. Not only can this help to clarify your thinking, but waiting to write about the literature until you have read 'everything' can easily turn the task into something unwieldy and unmanageable. Doing your own writing about the literature is the best way of thinking and learning about the literature. First attempts at writing will be a way of beginning to understand the literature, which can subsequently be refined, as more reading allows for deeper and wider understanding and knowledge. However, this also means that the writing you do along the way will rarely be the end product that goes into your final piece of work. (Again, Ridley (2012) provides valuable detail on note-taking and summarizing).

Talking about it

Reviewing the literature does not only mean going away, gathering literature, reading and writing in isolation. It involves talking about it, presenting it, and generating ideas and arguments through working with others. Sharing your ideas and learning from others in these ways can help to make sense of what you are doing, and give you an opportunity to develop your ideas and arguments in preparation for writing about them.

Summary: The key processes in literature reviewing

The processes that can be engaged in while conducting a literature search and review can be summarized by considering the following activities that are usually carried out by people during the process:

1   Scoping: deciding on the areas you will search, 'mapping' areas out, perhaps beginning to think about areas that may not be covered.

2   Searching, finding and locating: actually starting and conducting the search

3   Selecting: no one can read everything. This is where you really must be selective and make explicit the criteria for including or not including something. The selection is often guided and driven by the research questions.

4   Sorting and categorizing: putting reading into groups, mapping (again), deciding on categories (which may be arbitrary).

5   Evaluating and being critical: reading critically, making notes (see Chapter 6 for a full discussion)

6   Synthesizing, comparing and connecting: making links between the selected sources

7   Storing, recording and filing both the reading and your initial writing on it.

Writing about the literature

Build an argument, not a library (Rudestam and Newton 1992, 49).

Writing about the literature does not mean reporting on everything that has ever been written about your research area. The wide reading that you undertake gives you the expertise to build an argument, but this does not mean that all the reading you have done will be cited in what you write (Rudestam and Newton 1992). The discussion of literature should link in with your research aims or questions, identify key themes relevant to your work, and then engage with and debate the issues raised. Writing about the literature should be seen as a 'dialogue between you and the reader'.

The literature can be treated in varying detail. Rudestam and Newton (1992, 51) talk of using 'long shots, medium shots and close-ups', suggesting that some work can be considered in a broad overview, while other research is examined in detail. Background material may be acknowledged and referenced as part of a broad overview. Studies with most direct relevance to the research question or focus need to be examined carefully, with a critical examination of the detail of the study.

The writer needs to guide the reader through, by making their purpose clear from the start, that is, by not only organizing and structuring the writing, but explaining the structure to the reader. This should be done by clarifying your guiding questions or issues from the outset, and keeping to this focus. In particular, you need to explain how the literature that you are reviewing links to your own work. It is also helpful to explain what literature you have *not* reviewed, as well as what you have included, and why you have made this selection.

Some people find it helpful to use diagrams to clarify the literature that has been used, and to show the links that have been made between the literature and the study being undertaken. Figure 5.1 shows some different ways of 'picturing' a review of the literature. Some people like to see it as 'zooming in' on a topic, starting from a wide-angle view and eventually focusing on the key area (Figure 5.1a). Others prefer to picture it as three or four areas of literature intersecting, with some areas overlapping and the central focus being the intersection of all the sets of reading. This is shown as the dark shaded area in Figure 5.1b. Others envision reviewing the literature as a funnelling process (5.1d), which is similar to zooming in, while the process can also be described as piecing together a patchwork, suggesting that it involves weaving together a wide range of areas of reading, perhaps in a creative way. One of these

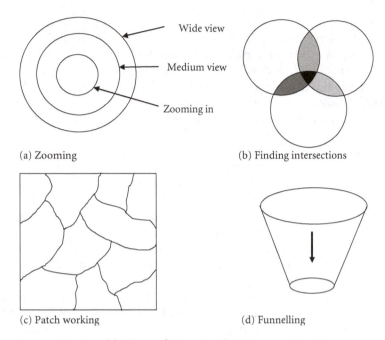

(a) Zooming   (b) Finding intersections

(c) Patch working   (d) Funnelling

FIGURE 5.1 *Possible Ways of Picturing the Literature Review.*

pictorial representations might work for you, or they may not. Whatever image you hold, or story you have to tell in your own review of literature, you should be able to explain it as part of the written account – and also during the *viva* (see Chapter 9)

The review can be seen as a story, which has key threads drawn from the literature, but where you are in control of the plot and the unfolding of the arguments which you wish to put forward. In writing about the literature, you are adding to it, by creating links, drawing attention to particular issues, and contributing your own construction of the 'story' which you have found in existing research.

Activities to engage in when writing a literature review

Above, we have offered a short summary of the key processes involved in undertaking a literature search and review. Here, we suggest that the following processes can be singled out as important in writing about the literature, using the metaphor of lower and higher gears:

A: Lower gear

1 Paraphrasing, restating
2 Summarizing or doing a précis
3 Describing

B: Going up a gear

1 Interpreting
2 Connecting (with other literature)
3 Contrasting (with other literature)

C: Top gear

1 Synthesizing or pulling together and categorizing or grouping
2 Being critical
3 Developing your own 'argument', taking a position, having your own voice.
4 Showing how you aim to 'build upon' existing literature (avoiding the metaphor of 'finding gaps' in the literature and hoping to 'fill this gap')

Practical tips: Do's and don't's

Reviewing the literature involves scoping, searching, collecting, selecting, prioritizing, sorting, reading with a purpose and seeking out key issues and themes – and then presenting and discussing these critically. The aims in writing about the literature are: to give the reader of your work a clear idea of your study; to provide a location or a context for your study; to convince the reader of your knowledge of the field; and to build a case for your own study – not arguing that it 'fills a gap', but that it builds on and adds to existing work.

The chapter has considered a number of key questions to ask when working on reviewing the literature, including practical issues of where to start, when to stop, what to collect and how to store it. The chapter has also discussed writing about the literature; the important issue of 'being critical' is discussed in the next. We conclude the chapter with some do's and don'ts which should provide a useful checklist before you submit your thesis.

How should you do it?

- It should be framed by your research questions
- It must relate to your study
- It must be clear to the reader where it is going: keep signposting along the way
- Wherever possible, use original source material rather than summaries or reviews by others
- Be in control, not totally deferent to or 'tossed about by' previous literature
- Be selective. Ask 'why am I including this?'
- It is probably best to treat it as a research project in its own right
- Engage in a dialogue with the literature; you are not just providing a summary.

How not to do it?

- Do not become preoccupied with the literature so that your own study loses centre place and is 'tossed around'

- Avoid catalogues and lists: Smith said this ..., Gurney concluded that ..., Brewer stated ... and Uncle Tom Cobley et al asserted that ....

- Do not stop reading until the last possible minute

- Finally, avoid being rude, disrespectful, dismissive, scathing or polemical; your aim is to show some critical insight. Be discerning: remember that the Greek word '*kritikos*' is often literally translated as 'able to discern'.

Points for action and reflection

1 Why do you feel it is important to review the literature in the area that you have chosen to research? Can you imagine any disadvantages that might follow by 'seeing what has been done' in your chosen area before you embark on your own research?

2 What is your own feeling about using Internet sources as part of a literature review?

3 What do you feel are the advantages and disadvantages of conducting a 'systematic review' of the literature according to certain criteria?

4 The figure in this chapter shows different ways of picturing or seeing the literature review. Which images could or would you use in conceptualizing a literature review?

CHAPTER SIX

Bringing your writing and the literature together harmoniously

The term 'critical' is widely used but rarely defined. The Oxford English Dictionary (OED) provides a good starting point for discussion. The Shorter OED uses terms such as 'involving or exercising careful judgement or observation'. It also includes the phrase 'given to judging', and the terms 'fault-finding' and 'censorious'. The latter terms connect with the more negative aspects of being critical, and the occasional use of the term 'critical' in everyday contexts when it relates to words such as 'judgemental', 'scathing' or the more vernacular 'nitpicking' – in these contexts to be critical can be seen as verging on being hostile, rude or confrontational. Our discussion and interpretation in this chapter are closer to the first aspect of the above OED definition: that is, the notion that being critical involves the exercise of careful, deliberate and well-informed judgement – in partnership with others.

The aim of this chapter is to examine the idea of being critical, to reflect on possible barriers to it, to look at the kinds of activities that might be involved in critical reading and writing and to consider the concept of the development of a 'critical disposition'. These qualities and dispositions are all essential in taking control of your thesis and in preparing for the *viva*.

What does 'being critical' mean?

The advice to read or think critically or to simply be 'more critical' is often given but rarely made explicit. As Brookfield (1987, 11) put it very neatly in the 1980s,

> *'phrases such as critical thinking …. are exhortatory, heady and conveniently vague'.*

So what is meant by 'critique' and 'being critical'?

What do people think that 'being critical' means to them?

We have held many discussions and focus groups with UK and transnational students in which we discuss some of the activities that they feel are involved in thinking critically. Here are some of their responses:

- taking time, holding back and slowing down in passing judgement;
- questioning, comparing; making the familiar strange … and *vice versa*;
- being positive as well as negative – criticism usually has negative connotations;
- questioning established authorities, strategies and policies;
- seeing in more depth; looking for another point of view;
- discussing, analysing, examining different aspects;
- scrutinizing; being inquisitive; searching for embedded ideas
- reading between the lines; seeing both sides and many sides; looking for a new angle;
- not immediately accepting. not taking things for granted;
- thinking independently; evaluating; balancing and 'weighing up' different opinions;
- searching for reasons and evidence; doubting.

Many of the above comments resonate with the discussions in the rest of this chapter.

Various published views on criticality

Ronald Barnett, who has considered in some depth what it means to be critical, offers a helpful definition, albeit somewhat circular, of the 'critical mind' and 'critical thought':

> The critical mind is, in essence, an evaluative mind. Critical thought is the application of critical standards or values – sustained by a peer community – to an object or theory or practice. (Barnett 1997, 19)

Yet, Barnett argues that we should do away with critical thinking as 'a core concept of higher education and replace it with the wider concept of critical being' (Barnett 1997, 7). He goes on to explain this notion. Critical thinking skills are constraining in that they 'confine the thinker to given standards of reasoning' in a field, while his broader notion 'opens the possibility of entirely different and even contrasting modes of understanding' (1997, 7).

Barnett suggests that criticality should be seen as occurring in three domains: knowledge, the self and the world. Consequently, three forms of critical being are possible, which he calls 'critical reason, critical self-reflection and critical action'. In the three domains of critical thinking, Barnett argues that a person can be critical of:

- 'Propositions, ideas and knowledge' as they are presented in 'the world of systemic knowledge'

- 'The internal world', that is, yourself, and this form is 'demonstrated in self-reflection'

- The 'external world' and this form leads to and is shown by critical action.

Barnett used in several places the 1990s image (ubiquitous at the time) of the Chinese student confronting tanks in Tiananmen Square, Beijing, as a classic case of critical action. Certainly, criticality in Barnett's first domain is a key attribute or disposition; the second domain also seems to be indispensable to critical research and writing, that is, the ability to reflect on oneself. This imperative to be reflective and indeed reflexive (see later in this chapter) is an essential part of being critical.

A helpful definition of critical thinking by Bickenbach and Davies (1997) resonates with this idea of reflecting on our own thinking and our thought processes:

> Critical thinking, then, is the art of evaluating the judgements and the decisions we make by looking closely at the process that leads to these judgements and decisions.

This is similar to Wallace and Poulson's (2004, 4) observation that it is 'quite acceptable for students to question the ideas of leading academic figures in their area of study, as long as they can give convincing reasons for their view'.

Jenny Moon examines critical thinking and describes it as 'a sustained and systematic process of examination' (2005, 5). She herself cites Barnett (1997) who talks of a 'critical stance' which is an acquired disposition towards all knowledge and action (discussed in Moon 2005, 7). This disposition is more than a set of skills or abilities – it is more to do with a 'person's relationship with the world'. As a result, it is not quite a case of teaching people to be critical (and certainly not telling them to be critical as many a supervisor has done) but more a process of nurturing, encouraging and modelling criticality in order to foster this stance. (Incidentally, Moon 2005, provides a full and practical account of how critical thinking might be enhanced and developed with students in higher education.)

One aspect of the critical disposition is the activity of reflecting on our own judgements, our own evaluations of evidence and our own thought processes: this is, quite simply, metacognition. Metacognition will also involve reflecting on the part that our own emotions, beliefs and ideologies play in our activity of being critical.

This need for metacognition (thinking about thinking), and then of course the need to display it, are in some ways reminiscent of school mathematics when pupils are urged to 'show' their 'working'; however, it may well be easier to show the steps in one's thinking processes clearly and explicitly in a calculation, as opposed to other reasoning processes which may involve tacit knowledge, intuition and even leaps of the imagination (in scientific advances for example).

In summary, I would argue that critical thinking has several facets. These facets include dispositions and attitudes as well as skills and abilities. The necessity to be self-aware, reflective and reflexive, and to display this self-awareness, forms a key element. But there are other dispositions and other skills. Being critical involves adopting a position of healthy scepticism, respect for others without undue deference, confidence without arrogance, caution without timidity and, most of all, fairness. It requires the ability to engage with texts and scrutinize them, to evaluate evidence, to critique methodologies, and to examine the steps by which others move from data to discussions and conclusions.

Two aspects to criticality

The business of being critical belongs to two domains: the affective and the cognitive. The 'affective' is the area of emotions, attitudes and feelings; the 'cognitive' is the area of skills, knowledge and understanding (see Bloom, 1956, on this distinction although Martha Nussbaum 2001, argues convincingly that thought and emotion are inseparable).

From the *affective* domain, being critical requires the researcher to have certain attitudes and dispositions, including being:

- Confident without being arrogant

- Tactful and civil or respectful

- Insightful without being hurtful or polemical

- Alert for positives as well as negatives

- Positive rather than negative (constructive not destructive)

- Open minded as opposed to narrow minded

- Fair

- Honest and reflective (and reflexive) about biases, prejudices, stances or viewpoints.

From the *cognitive* domain, being critical requires the skills of:

- Being able to paraphrase or sum up in your own words an argument, a study, a report.

- Collecting evidence

- Synthesizing evidence

- Comparing and contrasting evidence from different sources

- Being able to evaluate sources of data or evidence of (for example) their trustworthiness, their 'authority', authenticity or credibility.

All these skills and dispositions need to show through in the final thesis and during the subsequent *viva*.

Barriers to being critical

Two key barriers

Cottrell (2011) writes very helpfully of the obstacles, sometimes personal ones, which may stand in someone's way when it comes to being critical. She identifies seven but for the sake of brevity here, we highlight two main barriers: one from the affective domain, the other from the cognitive.

The latter stems from a lack of knowledge of what it means to be critical and a lack of the skills or strategies required for practising this, that is, simply not knowing what 'being critical' means or having a clear idea of what it involves. This chapter is intended to help with this barrier. At a deeper cognitive level, it stems from a lack of understanding of the concept of criticality.

The barrier from the affective domain is rooted in attitude: the fear of being, or reluctance to be, critical of perceived experts or authorities in the field; for example, an alleged leader in a field or perhaps a student's own tutor or supervisor. This may arise from undue deference to those who appear in print – but equally it may stem from shyness, low self-esteem or the belief that those who publish are somehow 'beyond criticism'.

Do people from different cultures face more or fewer barriers than others?

This fear or reluctance is sometimes associated with a cultural context in which 'respect for your elders' is seen as a basic principle.

There may also be a related (again, perhaps culturally dependent) view that things are either 'right or wrong', perhaps more prevalent in some domains or disciplines than others. The idea of 'epistemological development', discussed shortly, suggests that this approach to knowledge can be challenged and moved on from.

But first, is 'our' form of criticality, for which we seem to push, a Western notion? How generalizable is it? In the cultural context of a Western university, it is both accepted and expected that academic enquiry will involve questioning the work and ideas of others, and students are commonly advised to be critical or at least to be 'more critical' by tutors. Anyone's work may be challenged and exposed to criticism. It is quite acceptable for students to question the ideas of leading academic figures in their area of study, as long as they can give convincing reasons for 'their view.' But is the notion of 'criticality' culturally dependent? If so, then there is no absolute criticality – it is always relative, seen from a certain position or stance.

For example, the culture and the society a person lives in may well inhibit or even prevent their willingness to be critical, or at least openly critical. More generally, in any context, new researchers may be in awe of certain authors or 'authorities'; this can lead to deference – as in 'who am I to criticize X?' They may verge on fear of, rather than respect for, the power and authority of the published text.

We suggest that being critical should involve some humility - on the other hand, undue or excessive deference may equally be a problem.

Looking at oneself: Reflexivity

Being self-critical is a key element, that is, part of being critical involves being critical of our own thinking, beliefs, faith and knowledge, not just other people's. This requires us to be sensitive to and aware of our own biases, prejudices and preconceptions. This is part of the requirement for our own 'positionality' to be included in a thesis, article or research report. It is also part of the activity of epistemology, that is, being aware of what we know, how we know it and equally what we don't know, or what could equally be called reflexivity or metacognition.

It is worth noting now that to be critical of oneself and one's own research can be painful; self-critique is very hard to do. Finally, we need to be aware of our own language and discourse (the 'dominant discourse' as it is now widely termed) and how it constrains us. As Wittgenstein puts it (roughly speaking, though it sounds better in German), 'the limits of my language are the limits of my world'.

The business of being critical

Frameworks and guidelines for being critical

Eales-Reynolds et al. (2013) adopt and expand upon a framework for critical thinking put forward by Facione in 1998 and used widely as the basis for a standardized 'test' of critical thinking skills. The framework contains six elements and our *own* interpretation of these is given below:

1 Interpretation: this is the act of reading and understanding a source of data or evidence or an argument – and then providing one's own interpretation of it.

2 Analysis: carrying out a detailed scrutiny of an article or document, looking at its key elements and terms.

3 Evaluation: this to me is the crux of criticality and is discussed more fully later. Eales-Reynolds et al. (2013) suggest that readers should ask: Where was the material published? Was it peer reviewed? Is the writing based on research and evidence or opinion and viewpoint? Are the conclusions based on sound premises and evidence?

4 Inference: linking new knowledge with existing ideas; proposing new interpretations; drawing our own conclusions from data and evidence.

5 Explanation: the act of explaining our own reasoning 'clearly and coherently' (Eales- Reynolds et al. 2013, 9).

6 Metacognition: the business of reflecting on our thinking processes and how we may have arrived at our own evaluation, interpretation and inferences. This requires us to be

not only reflective but also reflexive, that is, to think carefully about ourselves, our thoughts and our positions and biases.

This is a valuable framework. We have already considered the idea of metacognition. In this section we look closely at the third element, evaluation, but first a few specific guidelines to the above general framework. We suggest the following activities are an essential part of being critical:

1   When reading an article, a report or book, always look for positives as well as negatives.

2   Do not direct criticism at the person or people writing the article, that is, do not engage in ad hominem critique; direct the critique at the text, the methodology and methods, the thesis (position), the argument and the conclusions – not the author.

3   Cottrell (page 85) also urges us to 'read between the lines' when reading critically. We should search for hidden premises, underlying views or ideologies, tacit or taken-for-granted assumptions, ellipsis (things left unsaid), and arguments not always made explicit. We should also aim to identify the '*non-sequitur*' (Latin for' not following') in the text, for example, a conclusion, statement or assertion that suddenly appears from nowhere: it is not connected in any clear or logical way to any statements that precede it. Thus the critical reader should seek to be wary of authors who 'jump' to conclusions or theories from their data. The next three short sections offer discussion and guidelines for evaluating claims, reasoning and evidence.

Evaluating claims: Epistemological and ontological

Being critical in an academic context involves dealing with uncertainty and qualified claims, for example, 'It may be that ...'; 'These data suggest that ...'. The reflective and therefore cautious reporter will be presenting small, careful and justifiable claims. As readers we need to be wary of publications or presentations which claim certainty, proof or causality, for example, 'This study has proved that X is a major cause of Y.' Thus one of the flaws to look out for in an argument and conclusion is the attribution of cause and effect between two factors when it may only be justifiable to claim that X and Y occur together (what the philosopher David Hume called 'constant conjunction') or they are merely associated. It may be possible to claim that two factors or variables are related or even correlated, but this is not the same as claiming that one is a cause of the other.

Equally, we should be wary of authors claiming to have made an 'original contribution' or having 'filled a gap' in the literature. (Can anyone be sure?)

As well as looking at conclusions from an epistemological viewpoint ('How do you know'?), the critical reader needs to examine claims with ontology in mind, that is, what is the author claiming to exist? Are they claiming that certain entities have some sort of existence, for example, race, class, autism, ability? If so, what sort of existence do they have? For example, are they social constructions or is the author claiming some sort of genetic basis?

Evaluating reasoning and argument

Being critical also involves looking closely at *reasoning*: Do the claims made actually follow from evidence or data? The key epistemological question in being critical is: How does the writer know what they are claiming to know? The examination of their reasoning will pose the question: How do their conclusions follow from their data? However, this is where care needs to be taken: the history of science shows clearly that scientific theories over the last few centuries did not follow *logically* from the data. They always involved some 'jump' or leap of the imagination which is not a logical step but may often be seen (with hindsight) as a great insight or step forward.

Thus looking critically at reasoning similarly does not involve looking for a clear logical process (certainly not deduction) by which claims are 'derived' from the premises, the evidence or the data presented. Rather, it involves examining arguments and discussions to see how they 'lead to' or support a position (a thesis), a knowledge claim or a conclusion.

Finally, Cottrell (2011) points out that flawed arguments sometimes involve false comparisons and false analogies, that is, claiming that one situation is comparable to another, or one phenomenon or event is analogous to another. She also urges the critical reader to be wary of emotive language in an argument or a conclusion.

Evaluating evidence

Cottrell (2011) also discusses the distinction between primary and secondary sources. She suggests that the critical reader should be aware of which category of data or evidence is being used and should go on to ask: How reputable or authoritative is the source? How current is it? In the case of primary sources, what methods and methodologies were followed in obtaining this evidence?

Critical writing

There are three aspects to being critical: critical thinking, critical reading and critical writing. Most often, the focus tends to be on reading and thinking critically, but the same skills, attitudes and dispositions apply to the third activity. Thus the notion of writing critically to a large extent mirrors the skills, abilities and attitudes discussed above in reading and thinking critically. In that sense, it involves both the cognitive and affective domains. In summary, critical writing can be said to have the following attributes, most of which are easy to preach but hard to practice:

- It is cautious and careful.

- It is unassuming without being too humble or apologetic.

- It presents a position (a thesis) and an argument which can be supported and justified (I prefer these two terms to the idea of being 'defended').

- Its claims to knowledge (epistemological and ontological) are made carefully.

- It is generous and ethical in reporting on, reviewing and evaluating the work of others.

- It pays close attention to the language it uses, seeking clarity (in short, it makes sense).

- It acknowledges the writer's own positionality, that is, it is refleXive, without being too verbose or self-indulgent; writers are sensitive to their own preconceptions and viewpoints (their 'habitus' in Bourdieu's terms).

- It is refleCtive in terms of considering its own strengths and limitations, focusing back on either the original research questions, the empirical work done, the analysis or the discussion and conclusions.

The practice of being critical: Actions and attitudes

In attempting to sum up the discussions and arguments in this chapter, we try below to present the practice of being critical in terms of opposite poles, some of which relate to our actions and some to our dispositions or attitudes. Thus criticality involves:

- Healthy scepticism ... but not cynicism

- Confidence ... but not arrogance

- Judgement which is critical ... but not dismissive

- Expressing opinions ... without being opinionated

- Having a voice ... without being too outspoken or self-indulgent

- Being respectful ... without being fearful or too humble

- Careful evaluation of published work ... not serial shooting at random targets

- Being 'fair': assessing fairly the strengths and weaknesses of other people's ideas and writing ... without prejudice

- Having your own standpoint and values with respect to an argument, research project or publication ... without being polemical or getting up on a 'soap box'

- Making judgements on the basis of considerable thought and all the available evidence ... as opposed to assertions without reasons

- Putting forward recommendations and conclusions, while recognizing their limitations ... without being too apologetic or humble.

In short, being critical is about having the confidence to make informed judgements. It is about finding your own voice, your own values and building your own standpoint in the face of numerous other voices, from the literature and from other places. Ultimately, our own view is that criticality is not purely a rational thing – it involves emotions, especially when cherished beliefs and closely held views are being scrutinized. Being critical is not only a skill but an attitude or a state of mind – involving honesty, respect, humility, morality, tolerance and empathy.

Points for action and reflection

For your own study and in your field, what does it mean to be critical?

1 Does being critical depend on your cultural background and context? For example, in the UK there are a huge range of cultures: Is each one likely to have a different notion of what it means to be critical? Reflecting more widely, does the same diversity of ideas about criticality apply to international researchers and students from different cultures?

2 What are the barriers to being critical? Do the barriers depend on your cultural background and context? Do international researchers and students, from different cultures, face more or fewer barriers than others? Is it problematic, or even unacceptable, for 'Western' tutors to urge students from other cultures and contexts to be critical in a 'Western' sense?

3 Is being critical enough or sufficient on its own? In other words, an important study or research project in the

social sciences may be a critical one – but does it make a difference? What contribution does it make? Does it take us forward, add value or have important implications? Can it improve the world we live in? In short, being critical may be a necessary condition or criterion for a research study – but is it sufficient? Does there come a time when we simply need to stop doubting and questioning in order to move forward and make progress?

CHAPTER SEVEN

How to coach yourself through thesis writing

Where do thesis writers get stuck?

Through her coaching work and through the Thesis Mentoring programme, Kay has met and worked with groups of thesis writers who had become completely stuck, were struggling to get started, or felt they weren't making as much progress as they want to. Thesis Mentoring is a sixteen-week programme which pairs doctoral students with a postdoctoral research associate for 1:1 conversations that focus on the practices of writing, reviewing progress, and unpicking thoughts and feelings about thesis writing. This helps to identify what works for each student, and helps them plan a way forward which is manageable. Over 350 doctoral students have now completed the programme, and from each participant data have been collected through their application forms, via mentoring field notes, and in formal end of programme evaluations. Kay has collected data on what is stopping participants from writing, and also on what works to help them get restarted. The issues and contributing factors described by thesis writers fall broadly into three clusters:

- Unclear expectations and responsibilities, and lack of defined goals.
- Lack of confidence and comfort zones, and avoidance.
- Isolation and hiding.

Unclear expectations and responsibilities, and lack of defined goals

In short, this centres on not knowing what you are meant to be producing, to what standard, or by when. Students often talk in the early stages of mentoring about feelings of confusion, and being unaware of multiple aspects, ranging from how much data are enough for a doctoral thesis, to the style, content and formatting of the thesis, to how much you need to write per day or week, to the actual due date for thesis submission. This extends to lack of clarity about what the data they have collected in the doctorate actually demonstrate. Students commonly describe waiting to be told what to do, not knowing where to start, working 'in a mess', or flitting from chapter to chapter without an overall strategy or structure in mind. Waiting for 'the time to write' to appear, of feeling they must complete all data collection or analysis before writing anything, is also very common, especially in the STEM disciplines.

> I'm unsure of the timeframe or the amount of detail meant to go in. How long does a thesis take? I don't really know what I'm aiming for, and so I don't know if I'm achieving it or not.

> I assume my deadline is September. No one has mentioned when it is. When I started the PhD, I didn't know I would have to do a thesis – I still don't really understand what the point of it is, what will the examiners be looking for.

> I feel much better after breaking the task down into little chunks and setting the deadline for each section. It seemed I had to know where to start.

Lack of confidence and comfort zones, and avoidance

Students talk of not being able to face writing due to low confidence in their writing ability, not being a 'good' writer, or not knowing if what they are producing is of appropriate doctoral standard. Conversely, they may feel confident in their ability to write coherently, but lack confidence in the data they are presenting, feeling they are not enough, or not good enough. Beware the academic comfort zones of data collection and analysis! Waiting to experience a feeling of 'readiness' is a common reason to delay starting writing. Feeling insecure in managing their interactions with their supervisor(s) also causes delay, with students' fear of judgement and criticism leading to unwillingness to share the writing they have been doing. Students describe feeling overwhelmed and panicky as time ticks away and they make no progress.

In my head my thesis is perfect. If I start writing it, we'll all find out that it isn't, and I can't stand that – I'm embarrassed. In three years, I've never had a 'very good' from my supervisor, everything is always just 'fine'.

My supervisor said he'd read the thesis only once. I've already used up my chance and now I'm not sure if I can ask again. I'm trying to do it on my own and I'd rather just leave than ask again. I don't want to show I'm stupid.

I don't even know what my data show. I daren't open my files.

I will start it. I just need to read more, I don't know enough yet.

Isolation and hiding

Physical isolation is a common complaint with some students choosing to stay away from the research environment to avoid unwanted supervisor contact or feelings of shame about their progress. This however often leads to being cut off from colleagues and communities with whom you can test out ideas, check facts and discuss progress. In some cases, supervisor or department policy determines the students' physical isolation during writing-up time. Additionally, a second form of isolation is more intellectual, and more common in discipline areas where there is not a strong 'research group' structure. Students describe feeling that they lack interaction with other experts in their research area, and that they know more than their supervisor. Becoming consumed by their writing, giving up hobbies, friends and socializing can also be an issue as the student feels they must give every bit of the time to the thesis.

It's been months and months since we talked about my work. Now I just run the other way when I see her coming. Do you think I've left it too late now to open up communications again?

I can't work properly at home, there are too many distractions. The department office would be ideal – I'd have access to everything I need … . I don't really want to see my supervisor every single day, but it would be a better idea to keep me on track, push me on. Little things build up into bigger questions, long emails, there isn't enough time to even write down all the questions. A chat as you come in in the morning would solve this.

It dawned on me that he wasn't withholding answers in our supervisions, he actually doesn't know as much as I do about this topic and he was asking me to tell him about it. That was an eye-opener for me because I'd always seen him as a safety, a backup. I suddenly felt very alone.

As will be obvious to you, the three categories interweave and influence each other; for example if you are unsure what a good thesis looks like, and what you are meant to be producing, you will tend to feel less confident that you can achieve that standard. Or if you are spending long periods alone, without anyone to bounce your ideas off, you may start to wonder if you are on the right track and experience a confidence low. We recognize that these categories are not always as clear cut as they are presented here, and we don't intend to ask you to pigeonhole yourself into one or the other. What follows are three thesis writing toolkits, broadly based on these categories, and collated from the wisdom of the thesis mentees. These are designed to help you think through how you approach the issues, and identify some ways forward, and you can feel free to pick and choose from each to create a blend that suits you.

Thesis toolkit 1. Expectations, responsibilities and goals

The following are suggestions from thesis writers, to thesis writers, and they cover some different ways to reduce unknowns, chunk down writing, and start with the end in mind (Covey 1989). Think about the ones that are helpful to you:

1   Take a critical look at some theses from past students in a similar research area. These are available in the library and may also be around on shared computers or in labs or offices. You can then see what represents 'good' thesis for your discipline, and what the goal is for size, length, structure and style of writing. Ask yourself what similar sections will you have, what's different to your work, and what's missing.

2   Take a minute to add up how many working days are left until your deadline. (Don't forget to give yourself a day or two off each week if you can.) Be realistic, and minus any holidays, and days you know you won't write, for example, your birthday and family events. Write that number down. Then minus another five days for formatting, printing and binding. Now, estimate (and this will be a rough estimate) how many words have you still have left to write (check your own institution rules for thesis length) and write this number down too. If you divide the number of words by the number of remaining days, you get a rough idea of the rate you need to be writing at daily, in order to reach your deadline. This will change as you go, you are likely to speed up, and you might want to also factor in feedback and redrafting time, so keep an eye on your plan and adjust where needed. See Chapter 4 for more on creating plans that you can stick to.

3   Instead of planning way in advance, go through your diary at the start of each coming week or fortnight and identify 5–10 slots of 30 min–1h and save them for writing. Don't wait for full days or weeks to be free, but weave writing in around the other things you need to do. Write the thesis alongside and around other work and life, and take advantage of all the small sections of down time. Give each small slot a very specific focus, for example, draft 300 words on topic X rather than just labelling it 'writing'. This is known as snack writing, and writing to prompts, and Murray and Moore (2006) have written much more on these ideas.

4   Don't get stuck in the data collection or analysis comfort zone, telling yourself you have to finish it all before you can move on to writing – it's not true. Recognize it as procrastination. That's what it is! If you start to write now, any gaps in analysis or missing pieces of data will become really obvious later, and you will be able to go and fill the gaps to order, rather than collecting data or repeating analyses that you don't need.

5   It's really down to you to own your goals or plans of action and to own up to what you have and haven't done and face up to it. It feels better to produce the plan yourself and then negotiate agreement with your supervisor(s) rather than waiting to be told what to do next. It feels better to give in work that is only 80–90 per cent finished and accept that it will need work, than to be chased down on it while you try to make it perfect.

6   Initiate a conversation with your supervisor as soon as you can – define how to work together, what turnaround time is possible for writing, feedback and corrections, and how to balance other commitments etc. Are you working with multiple supervisors? Define with them the process of giving work to them. Decide as a team who reads which pieces and how to keep everyone informed of feedback and progress. Keep everyone in the loop. (See more on aligning with supervisors in Chapter 1.)

7   Leave yourself breadcrumbs in your writing. It's ok to flit about from chapter to chapter as long as you are nudging them forward incrementally, but leave yourself a note documenting what point you reached, so you don't waste time when you next open the file.

Thesis toolkit 2. Confidence, comfort zones and avoidance

The following are suggestions from thesis writers, to thesis writers, and cover some different ways to develop your confidence and to reduce negative thoughts and feelings. Consider the ones that would be helpful to you:

1   Just decide to get it written and go and start (or restart) the process today, it's not as bad, once you get going, as the anticipation and worrying about it. You'll never become 'ready' to write if you don't get yourself ready, and you do that by building up your writing experience. It's OK to feel like you don't know what you're doing at first, the more you work on the thesis the easier it becomes; you learn how to write a thesis on the job, not on a course (more on getting started in Chapter 3).

2   Divide tasks into an 'easy list' and a 'hard list', and do the easy jobs when you're tired, and the hard jobs when you're fresh.

3   Writing is a form of thinking that you will find difficult to do inside your head. In your mind there are so many facts and ideas, and each one links to all the other facts and ideas you have. The thesis in your head is a 3D network of connected fragments. The thesis you have to submit however is a linear document with a beginning, middle and an end. In order to see your doctorate as a linear story, you have to start to write it, putting down each fragment and then moving them around into a coherent order. At some point you realize what story you're telling, and at that point it changes and you can see the roadmap to the end.

4   Draft first, polish later. And keep a 'rough work' file rather than delete your writing, as you might need it back later.

5   Once you have started, stay started! Don't get frightened off at the start and end up have long gaps between writing. Stay on track and every time you notice you have moved off track, just remind yourself to come back. If you are sitting at your computer and your brain tries to make you stop and do something else, just bring it back. If your brain tries to give up 100 times, just bring it back 100 times. Use writing times for writing, and break times for breaks.

6   Talk to other students or postdocs if you can and ask them to read your writing before sending it in for supervisor feedback. That way you get friendly feedback on the small errors and basic sense, and your supervisor's time isn't wasted on typos, leaving them capacity for more involved

feedback. Perhaps reciprocate this and proofread their work for them – you gain confidence and understanding from seeing other people's work in progress as well as in finished form.

7   Find at least one person who tells you that you *can* do it. It makes a difference to hear that you are expected to succeed, and you'll get there, rather than always hearing 'if you finish'. If no one else, you can be the person who tells you that you can do it!

8   Make sure you have a 'go to' positive thought that you can use to push the 'I can't do it' voice out of your head. We can only think one thought at once, and you need to be ready for when these thoughts automatically pop into your head. Maybe you could keep a photo on your desktop that reminds you of a time you succeeded. Or maybe you could keep a running total of your word count or finished sections, or a list of what you will be able to do once the thesis is out of the way.

9   Check that you are breathing properly, all the way in, and all the way out. Keep breathing!

10   You don't have to change the world to get a doctorate, rather you have to make a contribution. If your data make some contribution to original research, then all you need to do in your thesis is show how you have got there.

11   You don't have to 'finish' your research. Your thesis is a status update on where you are at with the research, and it captures a point in time. There is plenty of room in the discussion to talk about limits, limitations, caveats and what would come next for the project.

12   Trouble discussing your own findings? Make a table to help discuss each point of your data in context. Columns: (1) What (What's your result? What are the limitations?), (2) So what (What does it mean? Why is that important? Who agrees with you and why? Who disagrees with you and why?), (3) Now what (What is still unknown?) (More in Chapter 5 and see the accompanying Coaching Tools here: http://www.sheffield.ac.uk/ris/ecr/mentoring/thesistools for a blank template you can use).

13   Worried what your data show? The fear only lasts until you have opened the files and looked at the data! Get the files out and deal with it, stop hiding because it prolongs the pain. You can do this!

14   Initiate your supervisory meetings, make contact, keep in touch, set agendas, feel in control, and don't wait to be chased down and feel guilty.

15   The point of getting feedback or corrections on your writing is to learn something, so expect to learn something. Don't expect to be told you're perfect – this isn't going to happen. If it helps, see it as a way of getting free work done on your thesis. Get feedback early so you don't make the same mistake over and over again (more on getting and responding to feedback in the later sections of this chapter).

16   Avoid sitting staring at a blank document. You could make voice recordings of your thoughts and then transcribe them for a starting point you can edit and correct. Try starting the next chapter before finishing the last one, it means you don't have a low point after completing a section where the panic sets in again. You have a work in progress which you can pick up.

17   Let good enough be good enough; there's a perfect thesis and there is a finished thesis – one of those is fictional!

Thesis toolkit 3. Isolation, hiding and reconnection

The following are suggestions from thesis writers, to thesis writers, and cover some different ways to stay connected to your research community and to other groups, and for making your working space a productive one. Think about the ones that are helpful to you:

1   Keep in contact with your supervisor as much as you can, you just can't do it without them. There is a shared goal for you both here, you both want you to finish the doctorate

successfully. Supervisors get very frustrated and anxious about chasing and hiding patterns too, so you can be sure that if you break this cycle you are doing everyone a favour, but most importantly, yourself.

2   If you set a deadline to send work and you aren't going to make it, just send your work anyway and explain what stage it's at. It's really tempting to delay until you feel you've got something better, but don't forget you can continue to work on it after you send it. Keeping to the deadlines anyway shows that you are making progress, and it keeps the conversation going between you and your supervisor.

3   Find the right location for you to work, not just the most obvious location. Notice where you are able to get most done, and go with it. Is it single locations where you can build a base that suits you best, or do you benefit from variety? Can you make your writing kit portable so you can move around and be ready to write whenever you get a spare half hour?

4   If at all possible, try to be physically in your department for some of the week, perhaps you could negotiate a day, or half a day, to be there. If you are around you can keep in touch, have conversations with colleagues and keep up momentum. If you don't have an office, does your dept. have a cafe? Or meeting or seminar rooms you could book for a couple of hours a week?

5   Join, or create, groups or networks with other thesis writers – even a micro-network will do, a writing buddy or a small group of you. You could spend some time each week writing together, or just meeting to discuss your progress. You could offer reciprocal proofreading services, or you could create a space to explain what you are writing, and talk it through out loud (more on using groups and networks in Chapter 4).

6   Keep talking about your writing and how you feel with others, talking it through often helps you clarify and get past problems and sticking points. In explaining the problem to another person, sometimes the solution becomes apparent.

7   If you aren't anywhere near your department or peers, you can use a social media site such as Twitter to feel more

connected and to find other people who are going through what you are. You can ask questions, read blogs and join discussions. This makes you feel part of a community of writers (more in Chapter 4).

8   You might want to make agreements with friends and family about what you do and don't have time to do while writing, and ask them to help you get finished by not tempting you with invitations, or making you feel guilty for being less available. However, beware of becoming consumed by thesis writing and losing your sense of self-worth in it. Set a maximum number of writing hours and stick to that number. You can pare back, but don't totally give up all your hobbies and lifestyle, be balanced, unwind and relax, don't get exhausted. Treat your thesis like a job and as often as you can, go home at the end of the day (more on balance and burnout later in this chapter).

If you're working at home, keep most of your home as a space for relaxing in, and confine the thesis to a particular area, ideally one you can close the door on when you are finished for the day. Otherwise it is very hard to get away from thoughts of writing, and guilt about not writing, and it takes over your life. Never write in bed or your brain learns that's a space for thinking about the thesis! Try taking a short walk after you finish writing for the day, as if you're walking home from work and leaving it behind. Try and make a sense of spatial or temporal separation of writing and the rest of your life.

Negotiating the feedback process

Getting good quality comments on your writing from your supervisor is an important way of learning how to go about putting a doctoral thesis together. As you can imagine, it's a key way of improving the criticality and flow of your writing work too. Getting a second perspective on things you are very close to helps you to understand how clear your writing is, and how well the points you are making come across. Things that may seem obvious to you because you are very familiar and experienced with them may actually be fairly difficult to describe or explain to an outsider, and may be interpreted in different ways. Leaving as little margin as possible for your examiners to be confused about what you've done, or what your findings show, will pay off when you meet them in the *viva* and have to run this by them in person.

Getting the supervisory feedback you need will not only help you describe your own research findings clearly, but it will also help you to critically position your arguments in a way the examiners will understand them, that is to say whether or not the context and the conventions are right for the discipline area. Each broad discipline has its own ways of doing things, and its own discourses, and to write within the regulations of that discipline is just something you have to learn to do. Your supervisor's opinion then is important as a more experienced contributor to that (broad if not specific) discourse. Add to this their experience of the various conventions and regulations of writing and submitting a thesis within the guidelines of your particular university, and they make a good ally for writing ... but you must strive to get what you need.

My supervisors have never asked for anything written ... in supervision I could talk about what I was doing, but they never saw anything written really. I think early feedback would have been useful, I should have send drafts in at the earliest opportunity

An assumption we're making here is that supervisor feedback will be both forthcoming, and useable. Ideally the feedback you receive will be thoughtfully given, and designed to help you learn and apply the learning to the rest of your writing. We are aware from our own experiences, though, that not all doctoral students have easy access to this support, and not all exchanges of feedback are as developmental and motivational as we might appear to suggest above.

Below we suggest a way in which you could guide your supervisor to offer you the kind of feedback you can use to shape your work. Even the most supporting and willing supervisor has a busy job to do and many demands on their time, and will thank you for thinking these things through and making it easier for them. We provide a loose template that you can adapt and flex to fit your circumstances and supervision team. Treat this as a negotiation process rather than a list of demands; don't get bound up by the process, and keep the lines of communication open.

My co-supervisors have fairly different expectations: one expects me to finish in about 3 months, the other expects it to take far longer. I don't know who to believe!

My main supervisor had been really helpful in the feedback he gave on my writing. However, I was sometimes torn as to whether I should consult my second supervisor or not, for fear they may have different ways of doing things. In hindsight it was up to me to join the dots, I should have kept pushing for clarity from them as a pair not as individuals.

1   **Agree a timeline for writing.** It's crucial that you reach agreement on what will be done and when, with the people whose support and time you are going to be drawing upon. As well as planning to generate the text at a writing pace you can manage, get a sense of how long your supervisor will need to read and prepare comments for you. What's a reasonable turnaround time for feedback on a page of your writing? And how long for ten pages? And how long for a chapter? Agree also if they want it a chapter at a time or in smaller chunks. If you have multiple supervisors, to whom will you send it first, and how will you keep the other(s) informed of progress? Or are you dividing up different subject-area responsibilities between different supervisors? If so, how will you bring the separate sections together?

2   **Write it.** As you will expect your supervisors to do also, be prepared to put in effort to meet the commitment you have made to your section or chapter deadlines. If you get off track with the plan for whatever reason, keep in touch with your supervisors and let them know why, and when the work can be done by. No one likes to be left waiting, not knowing when to expect work they need to plan for.

3   **Check it.** Sense check the draft you are about to ask for feedback on. As a minimum give it a read through and take out the typos and formatting errors. It's a source of supervisor frustration that students send work for feedback with variations on the note 'don't worry about typos and grammar, just look at content', because writing with a lot of

English language, formatting or grammatical issues is hard to process and provides distraction from the story you are telling in the writing. We suggest that if you can, you find a writing buddy, perhaps another thesis writer if you can, to read through the work and get rid of the easy mistakes. A reciprocal arrangement can benefit you both if you get together with another doctoral student to share and check each other's work.

4   **Send it.** When you give the work over to be read, make sure you give some context info about what exactly you are presenting for feedback. This might include what part of the thesis is included and what stage the work is at: is it a finished draft for checking, a first attempt or a work in progress? If there are particular parts absent or still to do, make this explicit, don't keep them guessing. Request the feedback you need in order to improve the work. What type of feedback is going to help you to make this piece work better? Perhaps you want the feedback to particularly focus on the narrative flow of the writing; maybe you just want to check if your writing is stylistically appropriate and if you are writing with enough criticality, or if particular sections are weaker or less clear. Remind your supervisors of the turnaround time you have negotiated, and ask them to confirm if that's still possible in light of your requests. You could book in a future meeting at this point so you can receive your supervisor's feedback face to face.

5   **Get on with something else.** Refer back to your thesis writing plan (see Chapter 4).

6   **Prepare for the feedback.** Reserve a bit of time before the meeting (or before reading the emailed feedback) to re-familiarize yourself with what you are getting feedback on. As you read it through, no doubt you yourself will start to spot some errors, or want to add clarifying points to redraft and develop the writing further. Why not 'red pen' it yourself and compare your notes with those of your supervisor?

7   **Meet to discuss.** We realize not all feedback can or will be delivered face-to-face every time (or by every member

of the supervisory team), but we do recommend it where possible. We recommend it in the main because it's possible to hear the tone of voice in verbal feedback that is open to interpretation in written feedback. We can all derail ourselves by interpreting written feedback as strong criticism given in an angry or mocking tone, and this makes us defensive about the work, rather than open to what we can learn. We accept that even face-to-face, getting your feedback can be intimidating. Just make sure you get what you need to improve your writing. Take some notes, or if your supervisors agree, you could record the discussion so you can refer back to it later. An important aspect of receiving feedback is to be open to actually listening to it, rather than preparing to defend your work, or thinking about what you are going to say in response. Try to hold your mindset in an open mode – think of it as trying to literally capture all the details of what's been said. You can consider each point later and decide whether to accept or decline the suggestion using your own academic judgement.

8   **Get clarity.** In our discussions with students we have seen variations of 'I thought that was what my supervisor wanted' many times over. Particularly where meetings are rushed, we can tend to walk away with a sense of what's to be done but be missing a few vital details. As a rule try never to walk away without getting clarity on exactly what is to be done, because you risk wasting your time if you don't have the full picture. If the feedback is written, we know this is harder as there is no two-way dialogue about what's written on the page, but perhaps you could follow up with a phone call or Skype? Some questions you can use to get clarity in person or by email are: 'Can you tell me what you think would work better?' 'Can you point me to a good example of what you mean?' 'Would you prefer [option 1] or [option 2]?' 'Can I check I have understood that you are recommending I do [X]?' 'I think you are saying [X] is the priority thing to focus on, have I interpreted that correctly?'

9   **Agree on actions and timeline.** Factor in time shortly after the feedback has been received and considered to send

an email (i.e. get it in writing) summarizing what was discussed, the understanding you took away from the meeting, what actions you are going to take, and by when. At this point it's a good plan to copy in any supervisors who have not been at the meeting so that they are included in the discussion. There is also a possibility you have received more than one set of feedback, and this is a good opportunity to tie up comments from all people into an agreed set of points you can go away and address.

10 Redraft. Address the agreed points and email them back to all supervisors with a message explaining how you have addressed the comments they have given you. The most thorough example of this we have seen included using a table to signpost supervisors to page numbers.

I am now stricter with myself on my recording of outcomes from supervision meeting. These are invaluable as references to avoid miscommunication of requirement or responsibility.

A note about Track Changes (in Microsoft Word) and the use of this tool for giving feedback: some people find Track Changes useful, systematic and efficient for receiving and processing comments; others find it confusing, intimidating and somewhat disheartening. It's worth agreeing whether this will be used, and remember that Track Changes was designed as a version control tool, not as a feedback tool. In our experience, using Track Changes can lead the supervisor to end up correcting all the minor errors, leaving you the student as a passive recipient of the feedback rather than giving you a chance to actively improve your writing style. We leave the decision up to you, but if you find it's not working for you, think about discussing this with your supervisor(s).

A serious point: all of the above become redundant if the process fails at point 1. We have seen so many unfortunate cases of students whose emails go unanswered, whose chapters stagnate in in-trays for months, or who are refused face-to-face time for feedback meetings. If you aren't getting appropriate feedback from your supervisor(s), and you try the ideas above, it's a good idea to raise this as an issue with the designated staff member for doctoral student matters in your department.

Ups and downs: balance, self-care, and mental health.

Learning what makes me stressed has been very useful because I no longer feel negatively overwhelmed by my PhD. I have learnt to put things into perspective and I see my stress as something that is currently in the way and that I have to deal with. Once I have dealt with it, I can get back to being productive.

We declare upfront that neither of us is a trained mental health professional, though we do both work in roles where it is part of our duty of care as professionals to be able to spot students who are struggling with stress, fatigue, burnout, and other mental health difficulties or disabilities, and help them to locate the right source of support. We have seen the things we refer to in this section a number of times across different populations of doctoral students, and we offer the information below as a way you could become more aware of how your mind and body are reacting to the doctoral processes. Most doctoral students experience emotional highs and lows throughout the doctorate: the joy of discovery, the pressure of deadlines, the exhilaration of a breakthrough, the fear of the unknown, the excitement of starting a project and opening up possibilities, and the frustration of the final push to get the doctorate finished. Some thesis writers, especially if they have been working on a project with more downs than ups which is tiring, can get stuck repeating unhelpful work habits, negative ways of thinking or become trapped in frustrating patterns of communication, which cause them to experience stress and anxiety in the writing process. We emphasize that in every doctorate, self-care, making time to look after yourself and your health, taking breaks and taking time off for holidays are important long-term research strategies. Managing your energy budget for the long haul is really important.

Balance

UK government health advice for people in stressful situations emphasizes that we should take some time to ourselves, just for guilt-free relaxation, and suggests that a physical activity that involves some movement (e.g. running, walking, dancing) can calm us and increase our feelings of wellbeing, with added health benefits including burning off the adrenaline we generate in stressful situations. The authors echo this need to take breaks and find balance, and we hear from our thesis writers that other pastimes such as meeting with friends, playing music, gardening, knitting, gaming, etc. also can bring a sense of balance and provide relaxation, and by taking time out, you come back to writing feeling refreshed. Engaging in any creative endeavour, one where you can feel a sense of relaxation and accomplishment, can help stress management, as well as self-care techniques such as eating enough nutritious food, staying hydrated and getting enough sleep. We urge you to take time away from your writing and give yourself a break. You will only be able to sustain thesis writing for the duration if you take time to take care of yourself. You could also try balancing 'harder' writing tasks (those that need more mental effort from you) with tasks you find easier. So why not save yourself a list of easier jobs for when you get thesis-fatigue?

> *Do not give it everything you have, it just isn't worth it: go on that picnic, go to that reunion, etc ... the research will still be there on Monday.*

Time off

Each doctorate is different and has more and less busy periods, and more stressful, and less stressful periods. It's up to you to manage your time and energy appropriately to match these demands, and we encourage you to be flexible where you can to meet the needs of the research. It's easy though to get into an escalating pattern of working longer and longer hours as the data become more interesting, and you are juggling multiple strands of the project. If thing aren't going well, or if you feel you are behind schedule, it's tempting to try to remedy this by putting more and more effort in. Be aware though that working longer and harder is not a guarantee that you will get more and better results. As well as being entitled to expect reasonable and manageable working hours, doctoral students are entitled to take time away from their research, for breaks and holidays – this varies between research institutions, so check out your own student handbook or online guidance. (It is approximately eight weeks holiday entitlement including bank holidays.) This is personal free time you can expect to enjoy in order to rest and recuperate. Time off is a necessary part of doing good work, it is not a reward for making good progress. In fact it might be an idea to take a break, or set some work-time limits for yourself if you have become stuck, if things aren't going well, or if you are feeling stressed. In fact there is evidence to suggest that people who take breaks to rest, maintain their focus better by avoiding digital distractions (Wagner et al. 2012), and are more productive as during breaks they revaluate their work strategy (Auriga and Lleras 2011).

Resilience in the doctorate

Any learning experience, but particularly the doctoral learning experience which deals with a lot of uncertainty, will contain competitive elements of win and loss, aspiration and failure, application and rejection and trial and error. How we respond to the difficult experiences of loss, failure, rejection and error, learn from them, and adapt our strategies is commonly placed under the umbrella term of resilience. Resilience is a difficult area of study, though with no consensus on a definition for the term or on what attributes it involves, or on how we develop them. Some of the research available positions personality factors as most important in determining how much resilience we can individually muster (e.g. Kelley 2005), and other studies show that the social environment and how supportive our friends and colleagues are can also bolster resilience (Richardson 2002). In Thesis Coaching we talk about using 'feedback filters' to screen each review, criticism or piece of negative feedback in order to sift out what is useful to you, seize that gift, and move on. Some comments on resilience in processing harsh or critical feedback, derived from the thesis mentees Kay has worked with, are offered below.

> *Feedback is the data you need to receive to know things about yourself you'd otherwise miss. You can't know it all, and if you think you can it'll hurt more. Just accept that yours is one viewpoint, and you need others to get the full picture.*

Once I properly accepted, yeah, I'm a human who make mistakes, and writing about brand [new] research doesn't have a roadmap, well, I just saw that as a part of learning to be a researcher. Expect error, factor it in.

I tell myself that the feedback as free work someone is doing on my behalf. I ask for feedback and my supervisor does work for me, to help my argument be as good as it can be. I can utilize his experience, to get what I want, a good thesis.

If you look at it, the feedback you get is a nugget of good stuff, wrapped in someone else's ego. Unwrap the useful stuff, throw away the stuff that's all about them, and you're on a winner.

I used to get feedback and then get caught up in writing long emails to justify myself and my choices. You don't need to justify yourself, it's a massive waste of your time. When I think about what I was doing it for ... I don't know ... to look good? Because my pride was hurt? If I'd just gone, 'right, thanks' and moved on I'd have finished a lot quicker. Now I only get into a discussion about it if I don't understand the feedback.

If you need to respond, make yourself wait a while, and calm down. Then start with bullet points and keep it to the facts. Don't get caught up in arguing a point. In fact I always pretend I'm explaining the feedback to someone else, and even say it out loud, it helps me to get to the point where I know what I'm going to actually do about it. And that's what I reply, like, 'OK I'm going to do a, b, and c about this, I think points d and e are fine and I'm not going to change that'.

Taking care of your mental health

Specialist counselling services, disability services, and wellbeing services are available at many institutions, and so if you are experiencing symptoms of stress, anxiety or depression, or other pre-existing or emerging mental health challenges, it's a good idea to get in touch with them, or visit your GP (family doctor) to discuss your options for support. Writing is an emotional process (see Chapter 3) and can trigger strong feelings, but recognizing when this has gone beyond everyday ranges is important. The doctorate does not have to be painful, and you do not have to put up with prolonged difficult experiences in the name of research. We offer the information below in order that you may use it to become informed about how to spot warning signs in yourself and what you can do to take care of yourself in stressful situations. In compiling this, we draw on good practice guidelines from the literature, from the web pages of mental health support charities such as Mind, No Panic and from the NHS Moodzone advice available.

I wish I had been more positive, caring and understanding to myself. Projecting negative judgements on to myself has not helped me in the slightest.

Spotting stress

Stress is rooted in feelings of pressure, and we know that doctoral students can often experience pressure in the normal course of their doctoral work. Some pressure is to be expected as we work to deadlines and time limits, and because doing research is a process in which we are often working with uncertainty, one for which there is sometimes no clear way forward. Bursts of pressure can even help you to make progress in your doctorate by motivating you towards deadlines, and giving you incentives to achieve, learn and develop. This makes the assumption however that the pressure is manageable, that you have methods that work for coping with the pressure, and that you are supported to do this by others around you. When we experience pressure, we produce more adrenaline, which in turn has consequential effects of other biochemical pathways in our body. Stress can affect how you feel, think and behave as well as cause physical symptoms. Common signs of stress include poor sleeping, feeling hot and sweating, stomach issues, feeling sick and loss of appetite, difficulty concentrating, irritability, anger or short-temperedness, low self-esteem, fast and racing thoughts, worry, and the tendency to turn things over in your head. The limits and thresholds of when pressure turns to stress are therefore personal to each individual, their biology and the situation. What one person may find exciting and motivating may cause stress in another individual, as we all have different preferences for how we work and different experiences of coping with pressure. A feeling of control and creating a healthy balance in your schedule is a necessary part of managing stress. To keep an eye on how you are coping and managing pressure, and avoiding stress, some things to notice are below. Is the pressure of your doctorate meaning you have:

- Difficulty concentrating on tasks, short attention span, and trouble completing work on time?

- A shorter temper than usual, you are snapping at people, or you feel more agitated than you usually would?

- More tense feelings, you're experiencing tension headaches, and tight muscles?

- Changed your eating or drinking habits, for example, you are stress eating or comfort eating, or drinking alcohol to relax?

- Difficulty sleeping, are waking up frequently, or your sleep patterns have changed?

Burnout

Burnout, sometimes referred to as job burnout, occupational burnout, or burnout syndrome, is still a somewhat unclear condition, but it basically describes the negative consequences of working in conditions of severe stress and high ideals. Burnout was first identified in people in helping professions (where there is a culture of self-sacrifice, long hours, high expectations, and blurring of personal and professional time boundaries). The symptoms of burnout deal with our feelings about our work and include: becoming exhausted, experiencing cynicism and detachment from our work, ineffectiveness and lack of accomplishment, and being unable to cope. The concept is used commonly now across all types of role and employer to understand the consequences of prolonged self-sacrifice at work. A workplace culture that expects such high commitment that it leads employees to neglect their own needs (time off, relaxation, work-life balance, meal breaks) may be at the root of it. You can probably see the parallels we are drawing; some doctoral research cultures can make unachievable demands of your time and effort. However, you need to be able to sustain your writing patterns and the hours you are putting in, over the weeks and months to come. Your energy budget won't keep increasing to meet unreasonable demands, and remember it's not just people who hate their work who can get burnout, high achievers who place pressure on themselves to cope alone can also find this approach becomes isolating and unhelpful.

Spotting anxiety and panic

Anxiety is experienced as feelings of unease, fear, nervousness or worry. All people will feel anxious or worried at some point in their lives, and at some point in their doctorate, and as we all know, a small amount of anxiety can even help you achieve tasks for which you need a heightened sense of alertness and awareness. However, persistently feeling anxious, alert and uneasy is not just a regular part of life. It leaves you uncomfortable, drained of energy and can lead to tiredness and fatigue as well as other health conditions. Panic is a sudden and uncontrollable feeling of fear or anxiety experienced as a rush of intense physical symptoms (high heart rate, breathlessness, sweating) which can come on any time, and often for no clear reason. Anxiety and panic are not expected parts of the doctorate, and just putting up with it is not the way it has to be. Anxiety and panic symptoms are not a rite of passage to a doctorate. There are ways to manage anxiety and panic which can help you get back to a more comfortable way of working, and if you are concerned about anxiety or panic, your GP is the best person to talk this through with. It's worth keeping an eye on the feelings of worry, anxiousness or panic you are experiencing though, be aware of what you are feeling and how often. If you are feeling strongly anxious, or generally uneasy a lot of the time, or if you are over-alert, on edge, or unable to relax or sleep properly, or feeling tearful and needing reassurance frequently, it could be a sign that you would benefit from discussing the different ways available to you to manage anxiety.

It's worth chatting to your doctor if you find you are:

- Worrying a lot of the time, worrying about everyday things, and about things that aren't new or difficult to you, worrying about things that aren't really likely to happen, dreading things, or worrying about the fact that you are worrying too much.

- Often feeling like you are being judged on what you do and say, how much work you are doing, and what data you have got compared to others.

- Often feeling panicked, or nervous, have 'butterflies' or 'churning' in your stomach, needing to go to the toilet more frequently, having a reduced appetite, feeling nauseous or having indigestion.

- Often experiencing increased, thumping or irregular heart rate, hot flushes and sweating, feeling faint or dizzy.

- Stuck in patterns of negative thinking, or replaying situations that have gone wrong for you over and over.

- Unable to calm your mind or that it is racing in a way which makes you unable to concentrate.

Spotting depression

Life experiences, including the process of undergoing a doctorate, can elicit emotional highs and lows. Events, relationships or experiences we find hard to deal with, or difficult to live through, can leave us in low spirits, or in some cases can cause depression. A low mood (anger, low self-esteem, frustration, tiredness, sadness, being upset) in response to a difficult experience such as experiments failing, or publication or funding rejection is not a reason for concern in itself. It will tend to dissipate after a few days or weeks and is helped by talking the experience or problem through, taking action to resolve it, or making sure you are taking care of yourself, by eating and sleeping well. A low mood that persists beyond a few weeks, or is impossible to get out of, however, is something different, and it's wise to keep an eye on yourself and make sure you are getting the medical help you need. If negative feelings you are experiencing don't go away, or are too intense to cope with, or are stopping you from going about your life and studies, we encourage you to check in with your GP as soon as you can. It could be to your benefit to get some extra support. Depression symptoms to look out for in yourself can include:

- A low mood that lasts more than a couple weeks

- Feeling that you are not getting any enjoyment out of life, or that things aren't worthwhile

- Feeling lost, powerless or hopeless

- Feeling tired or weary, lacking any energy, perhaps sleeping more than usual

- Not being able to concentrate on everyday tasks you would otherwise enjoy

- Changing your eating or drinking habits, for example, comfort eating, or drinking alcohol to cope

- Being unable to sleep or otherwise disrupted and unsatisfactory sleep patterns

- Having suicidal thoughts, or thoughts about harming yourself

If you use the above guidance to keep an eye on your thoughts and feelings, or have any other cause to suspect that something isn't feeling right for you, or you don't feel like yourself, we wholly recommend that you investigate further together with your GP who is far more appropriately qualified to explore the symptoms and options with you. It's tempting to self-diagnose, but given the overlap in physical and psychological symptoms, talking things through with someone independent can really help you to get clarity about your health and your best way forward to manage your time in your doctorate.

> *Writing, for me, is a very stressful part of a PhD life. If you let it, this leads to a lot of procrastination and physical inactivity, feelings of guilt, and overall a love-hate relationship with the document. You don't need to let it.*

Among many online resources, the NHS Moodzone website offers tips and how-to guides to improve your mental wellbeing as well as information about available sources of help. It also offers eight audio guides with advice on how to approach common problems with mental wellbeing: depression, anxiety, panic, sleeping, unhelpful thinking, confidence and assertiveness, and problem-solving. http://www.nhs.uk/Conditions/online-mental-health-services/Pages/introduction.aspx

CHAPTER EIGHT

How to stop writing your thesis

Introduction

Sometimes the hardest part of a doctorate is letting go, and knowing when you have done enough. But you have to stop somewhere. We both feel that this must be a joint decision between you and your supervisor(s). It is not often an easy decision and is best not made alone. Although autonomy is often highly praised as an attribute of a doctoral student, it can be highly overrated if the word's meaning is shifted towards always being left to work alone. Why be on your own when you can consult others and work in partnership with them? This chapter discusses the meanings of your ultimate goal ('doctorateness'), the various forms of 'originality', the student's role in choosing examiners and some ideas on what makes a 'good thesis'.

What is 'doctorateness'?

One of the issues that perhaps we don't talk about enough is the question of what makes work of a 'doctoral standard', as opposed to (say) masters' level work or undergraduate work. What is distinctive about it? It is hard to pin down and make explicit the criteria that a student should meet in striving to achieve their doctorate. However, we do not feel that it is enough for examiners or supervisors to make comments such as 'I know one when I see one', 'it's all about gut feeling and intuition' or even worse that it involves some sort of hidden, tacit knowledge and therefore 'say no more'. We don't feel that this kind of 'shoulder shrugging' is acceptable.

We do feel, though, that it is difficult to actually write down, that is, make explicit, a complete set of necessary and sufficient conditions that would make a thesis (and of course the oral equivalent, the *viva*) of doctoral standard. If it had been easy, we would probably have had the definitive list some time ago.

In 2013, one of us published an article in which we tried to 'unpick' the notion of 'doctorateness' (Wellington, 2013). The discussion below is drawn largely from that article. So, if we try this exercise, where would we start? There are a few areas where we might start the search:

The purpose of a doctorate?

One way of looking at 'doctorateness' is to take a teleological approach, that is, what is its purpose? Some reasons may be *intrinsic*: the doctorate could be seen largely in terms of a student's personal development and her or his achievement; similarly, it might be viewed in terms of satisfying someone's personal and deeply felt curiosity and intellectual interest in an area or a need to 'prove oneself'. Equally, motivations can be *extrinsic* such as preparing for a future role or a future career; for those already working it might be career development; or it might be seen as a way of researching one's own practice. Some students (and outsiders) might regard a doctorate as a vehicle for a person to develop certain generic, transferable skills relevant to employment.

Process or product?

The value of the doctorate might be seen in terms of its *product*, for example: pushing forward the boundaries of knowledge; or generating knowledge which can be 'transferred', to industry perhaps.

Or is it largely about *process*, that is, personal development, preparing a person for a career, inculcating certain 'transferable' skills, providing an 'apprenticeship'?

Is 'doctorateness' found in written regulations?

A third important way in which we can explore how people perceive and articulate 'doctorateness' is by studying written regulations. All universities have documents with titles such as: 'Guidelines for examiners of candidates for ...'. Varying phrases relating to doctorateness tend to be used listing different criteria referring to different aspects of doctorateness. Some refer to the product: 'addition to knowledge' for example. Some refer to process: 'systematic study' or 'adequate industry' can be seen as examples. Some refer to the qualities or abilities or even dispositions of the student herself or himself: 'critical ability', 'competence in appropriate methods' or 'industry and application'.

The search for 'originality'

The two most common criteria that surface in both written regulations and during the *viva* seem to be:

- *Worthy of publication either in full or abridged form*
- *Original work which forms an addition to knowledge*

'Publishability' in the current era is a problematic criterion. There are so many ways in which work can be disseminated and made public: blogs, journal articles, vanity publishing and open access (where the writer pays), books, monographs, conference presentations and papers. So, the question is: Publishable by whom and where and in what? No thesis makes for a single publication or a book (unless you pay), though parts of it might prove to be publishable. However, the concept that poses most problems is 'originality'.

What forms can an 'original contribution' take in a doctoral thesis?

If we reflect on the quest for 'original contribution', we could list at least six categories and these are summarized below (based on a table first published in Wellington, 2010, p. 87) with a few examples given under each category.

1   **Building new knowledge** (various wall metaphors are commonly used here)

   ● Building on or extending previous work

   ● Putting a new brick in the wall

   ● Plugging a perceived gap in the wall

(Demolishing an old wall and/or rebuilding a new one would count as a paradigm shift – nobody expects a paradigm shift for a doctorate, unless it's Wittgenstein, Hawking or Einstein)

2   **Original processes or approaches**

   ● New methods or techniques applied to an existing area of study

   ● New methods or techniques applied to a new area

   ● Using a proven technique, approach or methodology but in a new area

   ● Using a new mixture of methods

   ● Refinement and improvement of methods applied to existing or new areas of study

   ● Cross-disciplinary approach to an existing area or a new area

   ● Testing someone else's ideas/concepts/theories in the 'field', that is, new empirical work 'testing' or illuminating existing theory

3 New syntheses

- Of methods or methodologies (see 2)

- Connecting previous studies

- Connecting/linking/juxtaposing existing theories to make a new compound

- Linking two or more previous thinkers

4 New charting or mapping of territory

- Exploring a new territory

- 'Discovering' a new territory

- Refining an earlier exploration

- Re-charting a territory

- Opening up new areas (e.g. those which are taboo) or neglected areas

- 'Clearing the undergrowth' (John Locke, English philosopher) to make way for further thinking or empirical work

- New samples or new groups being studied, for example, elites, hard-to-reach people (e.g. those not on any register or record; men who pay for sex; persistent truants); newly retired people who had previously been in high positions, for example, senior civil servants or politicians; or people who had previously been unaccessed or inaccessible for whatever reason

5 New implications for

- Practice and practitioners

- Policy and policy makers

- Theory and theorists

6 Revisiting a recurrent issue or debate. Bringing one or more of these to bear on an 'old chestnut' or a recurrent issue.

- New evidence

- New thinking
- New theory

7   **Replicating or reproducing existing work.**

- Place: Replicating work from elsewhere in a new geographical context, for example, a study carried out in South East Asia replicated in the UK

- Time: Replicating in a new time context, for example, work in the 1990s revisited in the twenty-first century

- Reproducing or replicating existing work with a different sample, for example, a new age group; a larger sample

8   **New presentation**

- New ways of writing, presenting, disseminating

We appreciate that the nature of originality will vary according to the field of study and the discipline, largely depending on how 'cumulative' it is, but these six categories are presented here largely to put your mind at rest on this somewhat nebulous, yet widely used, concept (see Wellington, 2010, p. 88, for other, personal views on originality and further discussion).

Your contribution

Where does the discussion above on doctorateness leave us? Each area reveals – rather like the parable of the blind men examining the elephant – different facets of the beast. Our own view is that to search for a single, common meaning belonging to all doctorates is rather like looking for the holy grail. However, we do owe it to students, supervisors, examiners and employers to remove some of the mystique and to make explicit some of the descriptions and characteristics that are often (deliberately?) left tacit and implicit.

From our own experience of studying for, coaching, supervising and examining doctorates, the single most necessary (though not on its own sufficient) quality that makes up a doctorate is the notion of a 'contribution', without the complication of the adjective 'original' or even 'publishable'. The key criteria would then be:

> does the doctoral dissertation have a thesis in the sense of a position and an argument? Has this thesis made a contribution to the field of study? Has it built on previous literature and pushed it forward a little? Does it provide another 'brick in the wall'? Will this *contribution* potentially make an impact – or bring about a change- in thinking and to theory, policy, or practice? (Wellington, 2013)

Thinking about examiners: The student's role

We hardly need to tell you that choosing your examiners is a vitally important part of the doctoral 'journey'; yet we are always amazed at how quickly people reach a decision and how often students are not consulted in the process. It is a decision that we, jointly, need to give a lot of thought and consideration to.

Your thesis will be read by an internal examiner (always someone from your university and usually a member of your department) and an external examiner (someone from another university – in the UK, almost always). The same two people will work as a pair in planning and conducting your *viva* and then in making a recommendation after the *viva*.

We strongly advocate students' involvement in suggesting both examiners; however, we feel that the final decision must be made by the supervisors in consultation with their colleagues (inside and outside of their own university). Staff in any department have (collectively) years of experience in choosing appropriate examiners – we should draw on this and on our knowledge of how examiners have 'behaved' in the past, as well as our own experiences of meeting and working with people around the world. We would not name names, but clearly we do not want external examiners who might be pompous, have inflated opinions of themselves, who talk too much, who could be awkward or aggressive, or who could arrive at your university with too many 'bees in their bonnet'. (Don't worry, these are few and far between.)

On a more positive note, several criteria should be borne in mind when suggesting examiners:

- Will they be sympathetic towards the aims of your research?

- Do you and your supervisor know their work?

- Have you met either the internal or external examiner before? (Do not worry if you have not.) Would you feel comfortable with them in a *viva* situation?

- Will they be familiar with and sympathetic to your field of study and methodology? (NB: the perceived national expert in your field may not always make the ideal external examiner.)

- Has the external examiner examined at your institution before? (If not, this may well be a good opportunity for us to involve someone new.)

- If your work is a professional doctorate, has at least one of the examiners examined a professional doctorate before?

- Is the external examiner likely to be fair, thorough and challenging, without being aggressive or overbearing?

- Will this examiner come to the *viva* with any sort of 'agenda'?

- The combination, or 'chemistry between', internal and external examiners is important: Will they work well together in planning the *viva*, asking questions and deciding on a recommendation after the oral examination? (This is difficult to assess, but it is worth considering.)

Once, having consulted the student, staff come to a shortlist of the two (internal and external) examiners and then approach them to see if they are willing and able to read your thesis and conduct the *viva* in the right time frame (Most regulations require a time limit of about ten weeks between submitting your thesis and holding the *viva*.). Normally, staff fill in the necessary form, which then has to be approved at faculty level, and the process can begin. You can then look forward to the *viva*!

What makes a good thesis?
Views from examiners

We have heard a range of comments from examiners on what they feel a 'good' thesis is. One (social sciences) recently said: 'It needs to tell a story.' In our experience some of the best theses

- Consider a wide range of literature (including at least one or two references which make the reader say 'Ah! That's a new one.');

- Are well structured and clear to follow;

- Embed their own work in the work of others;

- Deliberate on methods and methodology before their own empirical work;

- Are honest and open about the methods they have used, and why;

- Reflect back on their methods and methodology after they have reported their work;

- Contain few typos, clumsy sentences or incorrect use of words (e.g., 'effect' for 'affect', 'it's' for 'its', 'criterion' for 'criteria');

- Make explicit the lessons which can be learnt from their study and how other readers can 'relate' to it, that is, relatability rather than generalizability;

- Bring out their own limitations (without being too apologetic) and suggest areas for further research;

- Pull out practical implications for policymakers or practitioners or both;

- Contribute to the 'public store of knowledge' – even, perhaps, to the 'public good' – not just to the writer's own personal development.

How to stop writing your thesis

There comes a time when you can see the end point for the thesis, and the route to get to the finish has crystallized into a clearer to-do list. Now it becomes a matter of managing your energy and sustaining your willpower to get there. How are you going to make sure you hit that deadline? Our first piece of advice is for you to make sure you have a fixed deadline that you are not going to keep flexing or putting off to accommodate the temptation to keep refining your work. Most thesis writers will have a fixed and hard deadline, a requirement of the institution, perhaps a visa requirement, and probably also a requirement of the funder of the research. In some cases though, for example, in professional or clinical doctorates, part-time doctorates, or in cases where your deadline is self-imposed, there can be enough flexibility in the arrangements to allow you to slide it back if you want to. Beware this tendency to drag the process on longer and longer. For some of you there will be clear reasons for you to adjust your submission date, but if you know you have an inclination towards putting in more and more effort to make the thesis incrementally better and better, it might be an idea for you to force an end by planning a 'full stop' point. We have known students to plan in holidays or job start dates that require them to have finished their thesis. It's hard to write and work on something new, as many people who are juggling a new full-time job and thesis writing will echo.

That said, if you find yourself tempted to work 24/7 at the end to get finished, please remember that you need to sustain this last push and you will need to remember to eat, sleep and breathe, to be of use to yourself in this final stage. We urge you to continue to set work-time limits for yourself and give yourself a break to do something else. You will only be able to sustain thesis writing for the duration if you take time to take care of yourself. Planned time off is a necessary part of doing good work, and if you have become stuck, if things aren't going well, or if you are feeling stressed, an afternoon out by yourself or with friends might help you top your energy levels up again. Be kind to yourself, you'll reap the benefits later. In fact, now might be a good time to check in with any writing groups, mentors or buddies you've been neglecting or avoiding.

As you come to the end remind yourself:

You are submitting a work in progress

Your thesis is a status update on where you are at with the research, and it captures a particular point in time. You do not have to do all possible analyses, or all obvious next experiments, you just have to be able to explain why you made the decision to include/exclude possibilities. There is plenty of room in your thesis discussion to talk about the limits of your research scope, the limitations of what can be concluded, the generalizations or applicabilities which can be drawn from your work, and the caveats of your recommendations. There will be the opportunity for you to write about what you have left out and why, and what would come next for the project were you to continue with it. Are the gaps you feel inclined to fill actually gaps? Are they holes in your argument that render it unconvincing? Or are they additional work that follows up new lines of investigation?

Feeling insecure is normal

Remember that you are very familiar with and involved in what you are writing. If it's not a surprise to you, or exciting anymore, it's understandable that you have become sick of the sight of it, and started to lose confidence in its value. Remember that your opinion is now skewed and you can't objectively evaluate your work. You don't have to change the world to get a doctorate, you have to make a contribution. If your work makes an original contribution to your research discipline, then all you need to do in your thesis is show how you have got there.

Literature will keep coming!

When you are near the end of the thesis, it can feel like new articles are being published at an alarming rate. Repeated last-minute searching and checking for new literature won't help you. Like the multiplying ferocious heads of the mythical Hydra, it can make you feel that each time you defeat an article by collating it into your growing work, another two interesting articles appear and get on the to-do list. Don't be tempted to keep looking out for new outputs in order to add them; this will cycle and delay you.

The doctorate is a pass-or-fail qualification

This sounds serious, but we have not emphasized this to scare you. Rather we want to remind you there's no A+ grade available. A complete document which demonstrates what's been done, why it has been done, and that you have actually done it is what's needed. Think about what is required for a thesis and fulfil those requirements. You can't 'win' at thesis, there's no league table, and even your post-examination corrections (type and number) are private to you if you want them to be.

The end isn't the end yet

However long you spend checking, proofreading, polishing and rechecking, you will always find some small mistakes after you have submitted it. Not to worry! You can be doing these self-identified corrections in the time gap before your *viva*. You can even do another couple of experiments, or analyses, if you really feel they will be needed!

Remember that getting your thesis submitted on time is your responsibility and you make the decision on when to stop. It's your call, do listen to the advice from supervisors, do compare your work back to the good theses you have read at the beginning of the process, but the final decision is yours.

Below is a basic list of the checks and tasks for the final stage of thesis writing. Your own institution will have their own requirements for formatting, their own forms to fill in and sign, and their own submission quirks, so please do check them. They are normally available on a web page, or within the latest copy of your student handbook.

● Check the thesis formatting, for example, getting the layouts within accepted parameters, consecutive page numbering, creating a table of contents, a table of figures, and even a table of tables!

- Make sure that formal permissions for use of third-party images are in place.

- Gain permissions from journal publishers to include thesis content that is already in print.

- Think about how to diplomatically word your Acknowledgements

- Check the turnaround time needed by your university for its printing and binding services.

- Check if you have enough of the right type of paper and negotiated access to a decent printer.

- Check the location of the office where you need to submit the hard copies.

- Complete and sign your version of the 'Access to Thesis' form stating who can see the thesis, and any embargoes.

- Submit the thesis electronically to the online plagiarism-prevention software *Turnitin*.

- Try and squeeze in some time to plan yourself some fun activities to unwind post submission.

- Make sure that the latest version of your thesis folder is left in a place where the next writing-up student can find it!

Points for action and reflection

Before submission: ten questions to ask yourself about your thesis

We suggest that when you finish your thesis and prepare for final submission, you should have the *viva* in mind. We discuss the *viva* in full in Chapter 9 and also present a list of questions that we feel are likely to be presented to you. The following list serves as a useful checklist before you finally submit your thesis. We also suggest that you ponder upon the following ten questions before final submission:

1 Why did I decide on this topic in the first place? Why is it important?

2 (How) does my position, habitus or 'personal baggage' affect my research?

3 What methodology am I adopting? Am I using a combination of methods? If so, why? If not, why not?

4 Am I clear and careful about all the words, terminology or language I am using? Could I explain what I mean by them in the *viva*? For example, random, critical reflection, praxis, grounded theory, and action research.

5 What is the general issue of which my own particular study is one example? For example, transfer of learning or policy into practice? (This is central for the Literature Review and the Conclusions.)

6 What is my thesis about? What is my main focus?

7 What are my research questions? Are they answerable? How am I going to answer or address each question (consider them all one by one)? Have my research questions changed? How do they connect to my methods?

8 Which theorists, theories or theoretical frameworks have I used? Why these ... and why not others? How useful have they been to me?

9 What is my *contribution* to this area? What have I 'added'? What could people learn from reading my thesis?

10 How could someone else take my research further? What could they do next?

Your answers should go into your written thesis and will probably be needed for your *viva*.

How thesis writing makes you more employable

We could deduce the following from our combined experience: it can really help motivate you to get the thesis finished if you are excited to move towards something beyond the doctorate. That might be a holiday, a new start, more time back in your work role or more time with your family. For more than half of doctoral graduates, it's a chance to change careers and choose a new path. It's not unusual for doctoral researchers to feel drawn towards the chance to draw a line under what's passed and start afresh. This is a chance to review the learning you now have about yourself – what you're good at, what you enjoy and don't enjoy – and make a considered choice about your future career path. But, how can you demonstrate the value of your doctorate in a new role, and how do you describe your experiences in a way employers will understand? Below are some ideas about how just producing the thesis has made you more employable. These are easy wins, for example, for your next job application, and good to keep in mind if you're wondering why you are still persevering with the doctorate.

You have written a book

Contributing around 80,000 words on a topic makes you an expert communicator of the written word as well as an expert in your research area. You have crafted a complete and coherent story with a beginning, a middle and an end, which lets us know theoretically what you have done, and technically how, and very importantly why. You have written in a style that is appropriate for the reader and you have referenced credible sources. You have also created all the figures, graphics and images, you have drafted and redrafted the copy, and you have formatted, typeset and printed this according to the specified guidelines. If 'producing technical reports', 'preparing committee papers' or 'regular writing of management reports' is in the job description, you've got it covered.

You can combine an internal and external focus

In developing a significant piece of work that contributes your opinion to a global field, you have had to interpret your work in a much bigger and wider context. In doing this you will have used your entire range of foci. You have worked at a level detailed enough to spot the tiniest errors in formulae and chemical concentrations or that you can pick out tiny nuances in policy, tone or intention. At one and the same time, you have had to stay continually apprised of the latest publications on your topic areas, attending meetings and conferences to stay in the loop on new methods, developments and understandings. You have also had to think about what these new developments mean for your own project and your data, as a process of continual reappraisal and reflection. Perhaps you'll apply for a job that requires you to have keen attention to detail while also keeping yourself apprised of 'best practice' in the field. You can demonstrate this very well indeed.

You have managed a project

You can work aligned to a project brief, to create a deliverable work package, to be delivered to stakeholders, within an agreed time frame. You will have assessed the risk and the costs/benefits associated with collecting more data *versus* writing up now. You've planned your long- and short-term project milestones, managed your resources and the logistics, and quality-assured the output. See more on this in Chapter 3.

You can liaise with stakeholders and external authorities

Examples that show you can engage with external partners to move a project forward are ample in the doctorate. I make an assumption here that in your wider doctoral experience, at the very least you will have experience of liaising with colleagues in other departments, specialist services, specialist trainers (e.g. health and safety, occupational therapy), a funder, a professional body or learned society, a collaborator or contributor, a policy or charity partner, a patient liaison group, a school or community project. Have you organized an event, meeting, festive party or performance where you needed to make agreements or negotiate with the venue, catering, speakers, exhibitors and delegates? Through collecting data have you needed to agree access to participants, safeguarding, data protection, ethical approval, intellectual property, materials or technique licensing, have you gained any special permissions that enable you to access documents or archives, or to negotiate and agree copyright of images and published work? Each of these teams, groups or individuals is a partner or stakeholder and you will have some rich experience of what is often termed 'stakeholder engagement' in recruitment jargon.

You are skilled at influence and persuasion

A necessary part of writing a thesis is requesting the time and energy of others, whether to show you how to do a particular analysis, to read drafts and give you corrections, or to listen when you want to have a moan. To negotiate their help you are likely to have spared a thought for diplomacy in timing your requests and demonstrated reciprocity by helping others when they needed it. You understand the need to be consistent and reliable in delivering on promises and how that helps to cultivate trust. While hanging on to that a shared vision for the finished thesis can take teeth-grinding effort, you've negotiated and compromised to make it happen. This includes working with and negotiating with people over whom you have no direct authority. That may be your supervisor, your peers, technical support people, etc. This expertise could be termed 'upward management', or 'lateral leadership', or in some job descriptions is described as 'influencing widely across all levels and groups'. Now you know what the term means, you will see you are well prepared for it.

You're self-motivated

Taking leadership of a large and long-term project and being accountable for its delivery is a big deal, especially when there's no precedent for the project because it's an original piece of research. The thesis itself has been a project spanning months to years and you have shown sustained self-motivation and self-governance to bring it to completion. Through this you have demonstrated a commitment to finishing what you started, to stretching your comfort zone and to learning from your mistakes. You can now demonstrate persistence in getting it right and resilience in becoming stronger through perseverance. It'll be useful for that interview question on demonstrating your commitment to success.

You're a critical thinker

After all, that's what doing a doctoral-level degree is all about. You were regularly required to analyse and assess information from multiple sources. You are able to evaluate and critique your own work as well as the work of others, and you are practised at dealing with critical feedback. You are able to justify your decisions using evidence, without reacting defensively. In addition, your awareness of your role and responsibilities through the process of the doctorate has helped you think critically about your commitment to professional development, self-assessing your development needs and seeking learning opportunities, be that *via* taught workshops, mentoring, online learning or informally discussing with colleagues.

Technological prowess

You are great with technology and new media, from the packages common across employers, to very specialist software and platforms. You are likely to have experience of cloud working and shared file stores for collaborative projects, version control and data management. You understand data analysis, statistical and graphing packages and have handled large datasets. You can find your way around social media, wikis, intranets and blogs. You can understand how to use online and virtual learning environments creatively. Don't forget to mention all this; not everyone has had the opportunities to become proficient with multiple platforms and packages.

And finally, do remember throughout applications (especially for careers outside academic research) to refer to yourself a 'doctoral researcher', thereby avoiding the 'student' label. Some employers don't know the ins and outs of how doing a doctorate is different to being an undergraduate student. See how employable you are – good luck in your applications!

CHAPTER NINE

Finishing your thesis with the *viva* in mind and finding a life thereafter

Introduction

There are two aspects to the doctoral thesis and the examination of it: the written and the spoken. We have argued in this book that students should take control of their work while working in partnership with others whenever possible – the *viva* stage is no exception. There is no need to be autonomous in the sense of being totally independent or being 'left to get on with it'.

In this final chapter we discuss the purpose of the oral examination (the *viva voce* or live voice). We suggest ways of preparing for the *viva* and using the probable questions in the *viva* as a checklist before you submit your final thesis. There is life after the *viva* and we consider this amazing possibility; post-*viva* life may include (after a well-earned rest) further publications as well as enhanced employability and improved career prospects for both professional doctorate and PhD scholars.

Why on Earth do we have *vivas*?

The purpose of the *viva* is not, as some bloggers might have it, to put students through additional pain and torture or to 'rub salt in the wound' created by the long hours of hard work needed to produce and submit your thesis. We believe that *vivas* are a vitally important part of the doctoral process and that they serve very important purposes. Yes, they are nerve-wracking (unless you're a robot), they do provide additional anxiety and they need to be prepared for. However, there are several positive aspects to them.

Primarily, they give you as the student an additional platform or forum: as well as the written platform afforded by the print on paper and e-thesis they offer a new platform, the 'spoken platform'. They allow students to bring their work to life, to show the enthusiasm and passion that cannot always be conveyed by the written word.

They are also a type of 'rite of passage', an initiation into the academy as some like to put it (not our favourite term as this implies that examiners are in some way 'gatekeepers'). But it is an event and in many ways one of the most important events in a person's life.

One other small but important point: the oral event is an opportunity to show in a face-to-face situation that the work is yours – that you own it. Incidentally, this is often stated in the regulations of various universities, that is, that one key purpose of the *viva* is to show that the study has been done and the words have been written by you, the student. We know that many universities use plagiarism checking software (such as *Turnitin)* to show that there are no unfair means – but this is not as powerful as the *viva* experience in showing that you truly 'own' the work and that your personal energy, inspiration and effort have gone into it.

The blame game, the claim game and the 'O' word

First, in completing your thesis and in discussing your work in the *viva*, there are two golden rules about claiming and blaming.

Be careful not to blame

For example, all the previous scientists who worked on this phenomenon were mistaken; it's all the parents' fault; the government and policymakers have not done their job; these teachers are lazy and not committed … .

Be careful about what you claim

For example, my work is the most original since Einstein; I have found the students' 'inner voices'; I have filled a huge gap in the literature.

No one likes a show-off. On the other hand, there is always a case for claiming some form of originality (without blowing your own trumpet, of course). This is simply because there are so many different ways of being original as we have discussed in the Chapter 8.

These different ways of being original are all worth bearing in mind when completing your thesis but also when preparing for the *viva*. When answering the inevitable question about your 'original contribution', be upbeat without being arrogant. Rather than claiming world shattering originality or paradigm revolution, consult the list in the last chapter – you might then lay claim to a 'fresh approach', a new perspective, different interpretation, modified theory or alternative model.

Feelings towards the *viva*: positives and negatives

As one of us has written before:

> Many doctoral students, especially those who are "researching professionals," will be experienced at presenting orally during their own working lives. But presenting in the *viva* situation is likely to be a new experience and to offer a new challenge. For every doctoral candidate the oral examination is an important matter. (Wellington et al, 2005, p. 79)

It is hardly surprising that the *viva* is an emotional occasion.

From our experience and research (e.g. Wellington 2010), students voice a range of positive and negative feelings when they look forward to the *viva*. Here we have included a small selection (first shown in Wellington, 2010), focusing largely on the positives:

Positive anticipations

Feelings of the end, the climax – the start of a new life

Many students talk about the *viva* being the conclusion or my goal, using clichés such as 'the end', the climax, relief, closure, the final hurdle or the end product, with comments such as:

> *It will be over and I can get on with my life; It's a climax … a culmination of a long period of time*

A unique opportunity

A chance to get feedback, improvement and dialogue 'with 'experts'. The second group of comments tend to relate to the unique, formative opportunity that the *viva* affords, and the anticipation that they will meet interested experts, specialists or new critics:

> *I want to learn from it – I want it to be a quality experience*

An event of legitimation and acceptance

A prevalent feeling is that the event will be a form of 'proof', of acceptance, of approval, of admittance and achievement, for example:

> *It gives legitimacy, value and credit to your work*

An opportunity for clarification, explanation and defence

Many look forward to the event as a 'platform': a chance to talk, explain, defend, justify and contribute, for example:

It is a chance to improve clarity and understanding

A chance to show emotion and enthusiasm

The emotional aspect of the event comes through strongly with all students. Comments include:

I can bring my thesis to life; It's a chance to shine

Anticipations of utility and future development

For example:

It could help me build my career, and my publications, through contact with the external examiner

It could lead to publishing parts of it in a journal or book

Negative anticipations and feelings

It would be wrong to ignore students' negative feelings in anticipating the *viva*. There is a huge range but we have singled out only a few here:

Fears about the outcomes

For example, having to find the strength to rewrite

Worries about themselves before or during the viva

This tends to be by far the largest category of negative anticipation – students with worries about not thinking straight, who are becoming too defensive, have stage fright, are talking too much, and are being too emotional, too tired or too stressed:

> For example, *It's a lot of brainwork compressed into a short time – quite a workload*

Apprehensions relating to the examiners, their questions or comments

Fears about the examiners, their agendas and their 'power struggles' (perhaps spread by some of the horror stories that abound in electronic and non-electronic grapevines) form a large category:

> For example, *You don't know the exact questions that you will be made to answer*

Anxieties about post-viva feelings

Finally, a minority talked of their worries about what follows after the *viva* and 'emptiness once it's finished', with comments such as 'Where do I go from here?'

In summary, students have a range of views, feelings and anticipations before their *viva*, as the comments above, taken from Wellington, 2010, show clearly. They are all worth reflecting upon and sharing with fellow students; we also strongly advise you to consider and explore them with your supervisor before the *viva*.

Preparing for your *viva* – and finishing your thesis with the *viva* in mind

We have heard it said that it is impossible to prepare for your *viva*. We suggest that the only element of truth in this opinion is that it is not possible to predict the exact questions that are likely to be posed or the 'behaviour' of examiners, for example, which aspects they will focus on. However, if a *viva* is conducted properly and fairly (which, in our experience, they tend to be), then we can predict that a certain range of areas and questions should and will be covered. As a rough checklist, we suggest the following (adapted from Wellington et al, 2005, page 85) as probable general or 'gateway' questions, which may then lead on to very specific, more focused questions on what you have done, why and how:

General or 'gateway' questions that might be asked in a viva

Note that some of these questions would only apply with certain types of research, and are likely to be asked in this order.

General

Motivation: What made you do this piece of research? Why did you choose this topic? Why do think it is important?

Position: What is your own position (professional or personal) in relation to this field and these research questions? What prior conceptions and/or experiences did you bring to this study? How has your own position, background or bias affected your data analysis and your data collection?

Contribution: Please could you summarize your thesis? What are the main findings of your research? What would somebody from this field learn from reading your thesis which they haven't known before? What have you learned from doing it? What original contribution to knowledge do you feel that you have made?

Publication: Which elements of your work do you feel are worthy of publication and/or presentation at a conference? What plans do you have for publication and dissemination? Has any of the work been published or presented already? (Note that the practice of disseminating some of the work via (say) a conference presentation or a journal paper is within the regulations of most universities)

Your research questions

Please talk us through the main research questions that you have been trying to address in your work. What was the origin of these questions?

Theories and theoretical frameworks

What theories or theoretical frameworks or perspectives have you drawn upon in your research? Which have been the most valuable? Why these and not others? Which theories has your study illuminated, if any?

Literature Review

What has shaped or guided your literature review? Why has it covered the areas that it has? (And not others) Why have or haven't you included the work of X in your study?

Methodology and analysis of data

Methodology: why have you employed the methods you have used? Why not others e.g. X? What have informed your choice of methods? What could you have done differently, with hindsight?

Ethical issues: which ethical issues did you encounter before, during and after your research?

The sample: why did you select this sample? Can you see any problems with it? If it is a small-scale study, can you justify why so few were involved?

Data analysis: did anything surprise you in the data ('hit you in the face')? Any anomalies? How have you analysed your data? How have you categorized or filtered the data? Have themes emerged from your data (a posteriori) or have you had to 'bring them to the data' (a priori)? Why have you analysed it in this way? Could it have been done in another way?

'Generalizability' and key messages

How far do think you can generalize from your work? What lessons can be learnt from it by practitioners, policymakers or other researchers? The 'so what' question: What are its key messages and implications?

Strengths and limitations

Reflections on the thesis: What are its strengths? And its limitations or weaknesses (with hindsight)?

Further work: Which aspects of the work could be taken further? How?

What avenues are there for future research in this area, building on your work?

Open Forum

Is there anything else you would like to say or discuss that we have not asked you about?

One key theme in this chapter is our advice that when you finish your thesis and prepare for final submission you should have the *viva* in mind. These questions form a useful framework or checklist before that final submission.

Practical suggestions when preparing for the *viva*

From the discussions earlier about the *viva*, its conduct, its emotional aspects and its perceived purposes, we suggest that the key variables affecting the nature of a student's oral examination are likely to be:

- The written thesis itself

- The regulations of the awarding university

- The examiners: their views on the thesis, whether they have read and will follow regulations, their 'personal agendas' and the likely 'chemistry' or interpersonal interactions between them and between the student and the examiners.

- The student's frame of mind and preparation

The first two are relatively clear, at least in the sense that they are written documents, in a way in the public domain. However, the manner in which they have been read and interpreted, alongside the variability in examiners and their personal characteristics, is certainly not clear and is undoubtedly difficult to predict. For those reasons it can be said that every *viva* is different – however, that is not a logical justification for not preparing for a *viva*. Preparation is vital. From our experience, and from a reading of the literature in this area, we offer several general suggestions as a means of preparing for a *viva*:

- Know your thesis inside out and have it to hand during the *viva*.

- Talk to a range of others who have experienced *vivas* recently, but avoid horror stories.

- Be prepared to be criticized and challenged.

- Be prepared to defend your thesis and argue the case for what you have written.

- Be prepared to be asked to make (at the very least) minor amendments and possibly more fundamental changes to the written thesis.

This is probably the best general advice that can be given. On a more specific level, it is worth considering the list of possible questions given above. It is very likely that at least some of them will be asked!

Incidentally, it is worth saying that the types of question posed in the *viva* should be very similar to the questions that the supervisor was asking you at each supervisory meeting, right from day one. In both situations the questions will be about eliciting, clarifying, justifying, defending and explaining as in: Why have you done this and not that? What does this sentence mean? What have you done here? What are you planning to do here?

By preparing for the *viva*, students can actually improve the quality of their answers.

Good answers can clarify and extend points made in writing and can therefore often reduce the requirement for amendments after the *viva*. Equally however, our experience is that in some *viva* situations students actually explain or express ideas more clearly than they have done in writing – furthermore, they may even add or extend new important points, arguments or messages that have not appeared fully in writing at all. This is perhaps one of the ironies in a good *viva* performance – the oral communication may extend and enhance the written thesis and therefore lead to a request that this enrichment be added to the written thesis.

Taking control for the last time: behaviour during the *viva*

A student cannot control the way in which examiners behave during *vivas*, but in our experience the examiners tend to be civilized, interested, enthusiastic and open. Equally, the best examiners will be thorough and challenging. Remember that they have usually agreed to be your examiner because they have a keen interest in your research and they are likely to learn from it. They are not doing it for the money.

Neither you nor your supervisors can control the examiners, but you can control your own behaviour. The job of the examiners is to ask you questions about your work. We suggest that in answering these you are: thoughtful and reflective, concise rather than long-winded, and direct (without being rude). Do not be arrogant, defensive or dogmatic. The purpose of the *viva*, remember, is for you to learn with a view to improving your written thesis before it goes public. It helps to carry out some 'homework' on your examiners before the event, but on the other hand don't try to please them by contriving to include references to everything they have ever written. They will smell a rat. Your body language is important: don't sit behind a laptop, do make eye contact and don't appear to be laid back or blasé about the whole thing. It will show. Don't go in as if dressed for a wedding (or a funeral), but equally do not appear in your running gear or your football kit.

One final point about preparation: should you have a mock *viva*? We have mixed feelings about the value of mock *vivas*. Some students seem to value them, others simply do not want them and some who have had them come back after the final *viva* and say that the mock has not really helped. On the one hand, they can be a kind of practice event or a rehearsal. They may help to soothe the student's nerves. On the other hand, they may steal a 'student's thunder' and remove some of the spontaneity that is needed in the final *viva*. Equally, unlike the dress rehearsal for most plays, they may bear no resemblance whatsoever to the first (and final) 'performance'. If you do choose to have one, see it as an opportunity more to practice general oral skills, that is, the ability to talk about the thesis and respond to challenges, than to attempt to predict specific questions or to rehearse 'stock' answers. The list of questions above can be used as a checklist before you submit your thesis but also as a format for a mock *viva*. One final point – if you have a mock *viva*, have it **before** your final submission.

Thinking about publishing from your doctoral work – a few questions to ask yourself

First, we like to remind people that producing your thesis in print and electronic form and making it available to be read worldwide is already an act of publication. (It may be your first publication, although it does happen that doctoral students have published either articles or conference papers prior to their *viva*.) After the *viva*, when you have received the guidance and feedback from two examiners, we would certainly encourage all doctoral students to consider further publishing – indeed it is one of the criteria for work of doctoral standard at most universities and is often an area for questioning at *vivas*.

Our advice is to start by asking yourself four questions, in this order:

1 What do I want to write about and why?

2 What have I got to say and what is my 'thesis' or argument?

3 On what basis am I making this claim, argument or thesis, for example, from empirical evidence? from philosophical analysis? or from personal opinion and experience. (If

the latter only, then you are unlikely to get published in a refereed journal.)

4   Who is the main audience for my intended publication? (students, teachers, parents, peers, academics, governors, policymakers, other researchers … ?)

Having considered the above points, the big question then is: Where should I submit to? Making this decision entails an extensive study of the back issues of possible journals to see where your piece might build on existing knowledge and discussion. What can you add to what has been said in these back issues? Choosing your target is never easy but is essential. Seek advice on this from your peers and your supervisors. People, we included, have made plenty of mistakes on this in the past and wasted months as a result of sending an article to the wrong target.

And finally … Post-thesis: plus points and lessons learnt – the Transitions model

When we work with students who are nearing the end of writing their thesis, it's very common to hear them say something along the lines of 'I just can't wait to draw a line under it, and move on' or 'If I were to do this again, knowing what I know now, I'd be so much better at it'. This is to be expected of course, three years plus is a long time to maintain energy and focus for one project, and it's expected that you will learn and develop your research capabilities as you progress along the project. You don't have to see the processes of learning, problem-solving and optimization necessarily as wasted time though: you have had to go there, to get here. We are all changed enormously by our doctoral experiences, and taking time to review the value added by a doctorate can be a constructive experience.

Add to this that some of us are more inclined or well-practised in starting projects than finishing them, having more bursts of creative energy in discovery, path-finding and planning than we experience when it comes to putting that final twenty per cent into getting the project completed. This can make us impatient to get the thesis over with. If this is you, please be reassured that it's not a failing on your part, some of us just find it takes more energy to sustain engagement at the end of a project than at the start, we are not a natural Completer Finisher (Belbin 2007).

You may find it useful as you move from the end of your doctorate though to take some time to review what you have gained and could take forward with you from your time spent, sifting for useful ways of working that you can take with you, and letting any ineffective thoughts or behaviours go. William Bridges described these times of 'transition' as having three phases in his 2002 model, and coaching often makes use of his Transitions model to help people pause to review and to clear their head, enabling them to acknowledge what they have learnt and use it be more effective moving forward.

The Transitions model phases are below, and may overlap, especially if you are starting a new role, or settling back into and old one, at the same time as finishing your doctorate.

- The ending: We acknowledge that there are things we need to let go of as the doctorate comes to an end. It may be things we are sad to lose, or things we can't wait to move on from.

- The neutral zone: When everything is in flux, there is uncertainty and the way forward is not clear. The transition from doctoral to postdoctoral work can be like this and more so if you are moving to a new place to work, or moving out of academia entirely.

- The beginning: when the new ways of working feel comfortable, and right for you.

Whether you are at the stage of bringing your thesis to a close, are awaiting your *viva*, are applying for jobs, or are making some decisions about what's next for you, you can use the ideas below to navigate your way through.

Thinking about transitioning from the doctorate can include examining and evaluating approaches you have taken to managing and completing your doctorate, about working relationships, professional networks and the friendships you have made, about how you have communicated and been communicated with, about your development and your own role in that, about balancing work and home life, and about how you have chosen to navigate your research topics and areas:

1 **What is ending for you:** What ways of working have you enjoyed and are you leaving behind? What will you avoid if you can help it? What do you never wish to do or be involved in again? What mistakes have you made and learnt from?

2 **What is neutral:** What will you maintain, what worked well for you, what have you perfected? What positives can you draw from the doctorate (We bet there are hundreds of skills, attributes and experiences!), from meeting new people and finding ways to work with others, to mastering software or equipment, to how you now think about the world and your role in it? How will you utilize the positives you take with you in your future role, your research to come or to excel in a new career path?

3 **What is beginning:** What new ways of working do you need to understand and become familiar with? What do you need to learn to do? What do you need to find out? What are the expectations of the roles you aspire to? Which of you doctoral experiences can you use as a basis for expansion into new learning?

There is a life after the thesis that is worth looking forward to. So keep up your spirits in the event of setbacks or detours, you will get there!

REFERENCES

The Advisory, Conciliation and Arbitration Service (2014), *Guide to Bullying & Harassment at Work*. Available: http://www.acas.org.uk/media/pdf/o/c/Bullying-and-harassment-at-work-a-guide-for-employees.pdf (Last accessed 31 May 2017).

Aitchison, C. and Lee, A. (2006), Research writing: Problems and pedagogies, *Teaching in Higher Education*, 11, no. 3, 265–78(14).

Ariga, A. and Lleras, A. (2011), Brief and rare mental 'breaks' keep you focused: Deactivation and reactivation of task goals pre-empt vigilance decrements. *Cognition*.

Barnett, R (1997), *Higher Education: A Critical Business*, Buckingham: SRHE/Open University Press.

Belbin, M (2007), *Team Roles at work*, 2nd edition, London: Routledge.

Bereiter, C. and Scardamalia, M. (1987). *The Psychology of Written Composition* Hillsdale, NJ: Lawrence Erlbaum Associates.

Bazerman, C. (1983), Scientific writing as a social act. In P. Anderson, J. Brockman and C. Miller (eds), *New Essays in Technical Writing and Communication*, 156–84, New York: Baywood.

Bharuthram, S. and McKenna, S. (2006), A writer-respondent intervention as a means of developing academic literacy. *Teaching in Higher Education*, 11, no. 4, 495–507(13).

Bickenbach, D. and Davies, J. (1997), *Good Reasons for better arguments*, Peterborough, US: Broadview Press.

Bloom, B. A., ed. (1956), *Taxonomy of Educational Objectives, the Classification of Educational Goals – Handbook I: Cognitive Domain*, New York: McKay.

Bridges, W. (2002), *Managing Transitions: Making the Most of Change*, London: Nicholas Brealey Publishing.

Brookfield, S. (1987), *Developing Critical Thinking*, Milton Keynes: SRHE/Open University Press.

Caffarella, R. S. and Barnett, B. G. (2000), Teaching doctoral students to become scholarly writers: The importance of giving and receiving critiques. *Studies in Higher Education*, 25, no. 1, 39–52.

Cameron, L. (2003), *Metaphor in Educational Discourse*, London: Continuum.

Cavanagh, M. J. and Grant, M. A. (2010), The solution-focused approach to coaching. In E. Cox, T. Bachkirova and D. Clutterbuck (eds), *The Complete Hand-book of Coaching*, 54–67, London: Sage Publications Ltd.

Cottrell, S. (2011), *Critical thinking skills: Developing effective analysis and argument*, 2nd edition, Basingstoke: Palgrave Macmillan.

Covey, S. R. (1989), *The Seven Habits of Highly Effective People: Restoring the Character Ethic*, London: Simon and Schuster.

Chanock, K. (2000), Comments on essays: Do students understand what tutors write? *Teaching in Higher Education*, 5, no. 1, 95–105.

Cryer, P. (2000), *The Research Student's Guide to Success*, 2nd edn, Buckingham: Open University Press.

Covey, S. R. (1989), *The Seven Habits of Highly Effective People: Restoring the Character Ethic*, London: Simon and Schuster.

Delamont, S., Atkinson, P. and Parry, O. (1998), Creating a delicate balance: The doctoral supervisor's dilemmas. *Teaching in Higher Education*, 3, no. 2, 157–72.

Elbow, P. (1973), *Writing Without Teachers*, Oxford: Oxford University Press.

Goldsmith, M. and Reiter, M. (2008), *What Got You Here Won't Get You There: How Successful People Become Even More Successful*, London: Profile Books.

Hammond, M. and Wellington, J. (2012), *Key Concepts in Social Science Research*, London: Routledge.

Hart, C. (2001), *Doing a literature search*, London: Sage.

Hyatt, D. (2005), 'Yes, a very good point!': A critical genre analysis of a corpus of feedback commentaries on Master of Education assignments. *Teaching in Higher Education*, 10, no. 3, 339–535.

Ivanic, R. (1998), *Writing and Identity: The Discoursal Construction of Identity in Academic Writing*, Amsterdam: John Benjamins

Kelley, T. M. (2005). Natural resilience and innate mental health. *American Psychologist*, 60, 265.

Kovecses, Z. (2000), *Metaphor and Emotion*, Cambridge: Cambridge University Press.

Krathwohl, D. R., Bloom B. S. and Masia B. (1964), *Taxonomy of Educational Objectives, the Classification of Educational Goals – Handbook II: Affective Domain*, New York: McKay.

Lakoff, G. and Johnson, M. (1980), *Metaphors we Live by*, Chicago: University of Chicago Press.

Lea, M. and Street, B. (1998), Student writing in higher education: An academic literacies approach. *Studies in Higher Education*, 23, no. 2, 157–72(16).

Lee, A. and Green, B. (2009), Supervision as metaphor. *Studies in Higher Education*, 34, no. 6, 615–30.

Legislation.gov.uk. (2010), Equality Act 2010. [online] Available at http://www.legislation.gov.uk/ukpga/2010/15/contents (Last accessed 31 May 2017).

Lillis, T. (2001), *Student Writing: Access, Regulation, Desire*, London: Routledge.

Lillis, T. and Turner, J. (2001), Student writing in higher education: Contemporary confusion, traditional concerns. *Teaching in Higher Education*, 6, no. 1, 57–68(12).

Mackinnon, J. (2004), Academic supervision: Seeking metaphors and models for quality, *Journal of Further and Higher Education*, 28, no. 4, 395–405.

Medawar, P. (1963), "Is the scientific paper a fraud?" *The Listener*, September 1963, pages 377–8.

Medawar, P. (1979), *Advice to a Young Scientist*. New York: Harper and Row.

Mewburn, I. and Thompson, P. (2013), Why do academics blog? An analysis of audiences, purposes and challenges. *Studies in Higher Education*, 38, no. 8, 1105–19.

Moon, J. (2005), We seek it here … a new perspective on the elusive activity of critical thinking: A theoretical and practical approach. Retrieved from http://escalate.ac.uk/2041 (accessed 4 July 2016).

Murray, R. and Moore, S. (2006), *The Handbook of Academic Writing: A Fresh Approach*, Maidenhead: Open University Press-McGraw-Hill.

Murray, R. and Newton, M. (2009), Writing retreat as structured intervention: Margin or mainstream? *Higher Education Research & Development*, 28, no. 5, 541–53.

Murray, R. (2011), *How to Write a Thesis*, Maidenhead: Open University Press.

Murray, R. (2011), *How Survive Your Viva*, Maidenhead: Open University Press.

NHS Online Mental Health services. http://www.nhs.uk/Conditions/online-mental-health-services/Pages/introduction.aspx

Nightingale, P. (1988), Understanding processes and problems in student writing. *Studies in Higher Education*, 13, no. 3, 263–79.

Nussbaum, M. (2001), *Upheavals of thought: The intelligence of emotions*, Cambridge: Cambridge University Press.

O'Connell, B. (1998), *Solution-Focused Therapy*, London: Sage Publications.

Ortony, A. (1993), *Metaphor and Thought*, Cambridge: Cambridge University Press.

Richardson, G. (2002), The meta-theory of resilience and resiliency. *Journal of Clinical Psychology*, 58, no. 3, 307–321.

Richardson, L. (1998), Writing: A method of inquiry. In. N. Denzin and Y. Lincoln (eds), *Collecting and Interpreting Qualitative Materials*, 346–71, Thousand Oaks: Sage.

Ridley, D. (2012), *The Literature Review*, 2nd edition, London: Sage.

Rudestam, K. and Newton, R. (1992), *Surviving Your Dissertation*, London: Sage.

Taylor, S. and Beasley, N. (2005), A *Handbook for Doctoral Supervisors*, London: RoutledgeFalmer.

Torrance, M., Thomas, G. V. and Robinson, E. J. (1992), The writing experiences of social science research students. *Studies in Higher Education*, 17, no. 2, 155–67.

Torrance, M. S. and Thomas, G. V. (1994), The development of writing skills in doctoral research students. In R. Burgess (ed.), *Postgraduate Education and Training in the Social Sciences*, 105–23, London and Bristol: Jessica Kingsley.

Värlander, S. (2008), The role of students' emotions in formal feedback situations. *Teaching in Higher Education*, 13, no. 2, 145–56.

Wagner, D. T., Barnes, C. M., Lim, V. K. G. and Ferris, D. L. (2012), Lost sleep and cyberloafing: Evidence from the laboratory and a daylight saving time quasi-experiment. *Journal of Applied Psychology*, 97, no. 5. 1068–76.

Wellington, J. (2010), Weaving the threads of doctoral journeys, In Thomson, P. and Walker, M. (eds.) *The Routledge Doctoral Student's Companion*, London: Routledge.

Wellington, J. (2010), *Making Supervision Work for you*, London: Sage.

Wellington, J. (2010), More than a matter of cognition: An exploration of affective writing problems of post-graduate students and their possible solutions. *Teaching in Higher Education*, 15, no. 2, April, 135–50.

Wellington, J. (2010), Supporting students' preparation for the *viva*: Their pre-conceptions and implications for practice. *Teaching in Higher Education*, 15, no. 1, February, 71–84.

Wolcott, H. (1990), *Writing Up Qualitative Research*, Newbury Park, CA: Sage.

Further reading

Antoniou, M. and Moriarty, J. (2008), What can academic writers learn from creative writers? Developing guidance and support for lecturers in Higher Education, *Teaching in Higher Education*, 13, no. 2, 157–67.

Avery, S. and Bryan, C. (2001), Improving Spoken and written English: From research to practice. *Teaching in Higher Education*, 6, no.2, 169–82(14).

Badley, G. (2009), Academic writing as shaping and re-shaping. *Teaching in Higher Education*, 14(2), 209–29.

Becker, H. S. (1986), *Writing for Social Scientists*, Chicago: Chicago University Press.

Becker, H (2008), *Writing for Social Scientists*, 3rd edn, Chicago: Chicago University Press.

Belgian, R. M. (2007), *Management Teams: Why They Succeed or Fail*, Elsevier Butterworth Heinemann.

Boud, D. and Lee, A. (2005), 'Peer learning' as pedagogic discourse for research education. *Studies in Higher Education*, 30, no. 5, 501–16.

Bourdieu, P. (1996), *The Rules of Art: Genesis and the Structure of the Literary Field*, translated by S. Emanuel, Cambridge: Polity Press.

Brennan, T. (2004), *The Transmission of Affect*, Ithaca: Cornell University Press.

Can, G. and Walker, A. (2011). A model for doctoral students' perceptions and attitudes toward written feedback for academic writing. *Research in Higher Education*, 52, no. 5, 508–36.

Carless, D. (2006). Differing perceptions in the feedback process. *Studies in Higher Education*, 31, no. 2, 219–33.

Denicolo, P. and Pope, M. (1994), The post-graduate's journey: An interplay of roles. In O. Zuber-Skerritt and Y. Ryan (eds), *Quality in Postgraduate Education*, 120–33, London: Kogan Page.

Dunleavy, P. (2003), *Authoring a PhD*, Basingstoke: Palgrave Macmillan.

Elbow, P. (1981), *Writing with Power: Techniques for Mastering the Writing Process*, Oxford: Oxford University Press.

Elbow, P. (1987), Closing my eyes as I speak: An argument for ignoring audience. *College English*, 49, 50–69.

Elbow, P. (2012), *Vernacular Eloquence: What Speech can Bring to Writing*, Oxford: Oxford University Press.

Eley, A. and Murray, R. (2009), *How to be an Effective Supervisor*, Maidenhead: Open University Press.

Eyres, S. J., Hatch, D. H., Turner, S. B. and West, M. (2001), Doctoral students' responses to writing critique: Messages for teachers. *Journal of Nursing Education*, 40, no. 4, 149–55.

Johnson, L., Lee, A. and Green, B. (2000), The PhD and the autonomous self. *Studies in Higher Education*, 25, no. 2, 135–47.

Kamler, B. and Thompson, P. (2004), Driven to Abstraction: Doctoral supervision and writing pedagogies. *Teaching in Higher Education*, 9, no. 2, 195–209.

Kamler, B. and Thompson, P. (2006), *Helping Doctoral Students Write: Pedagogies for Supervision*, London: Routledge.

Kearns, H., Gardiner, M. and Marshall, K. (2008). Innovation in PhD completion: The hardy shall succeed (and be happy!) *Higher Education Research and Development*, 27, no. 1, 77–89.

Kumar, V. and Stracke, E. (2007), An analysis of written feedback on a PhD thesis. *Teaching in Higher Education*, 12, no. 4, 461–70.

Malfroy, J. (2005), Doctoral supervision, workplace research and changing pedagogic practices. *Higher Education Research and Development*, 24, no. 2, 165–78.

Malfroy, J. and Webb, C. (2000), Congruent and incongruent views of postgraduate supervision. In M. Kiley and G. Mullins (eds), *Quality in Postgraduate Research*: *Making Ends Meet*, 155–77, Adelaide: Advisory Centre for University Education, University of Adelaide.

McPherson, M., Budge, K. and Lemon, N. (2015), New practices in doing academic development: Twitter as an informal learning space. *International Journal for Academic Development*, 20, no. 2, 126–36.

Moore, S. (2003), Writers' retreats for academics: Exploring and increasing the motivation to write. *Journal of Further and Higher Education*, 27, no. 3, 333–42.

Murray, R. (2011), *How to Write a Thesis*, 3rd edition, Maidenhead: Open University Press.

Paltridge, B. (2002), Thesis and dissertation writing: An examination of published advice and actual practice. *English for Specific Purposes*, 21, no. 2, 125–43.

Parker, R. (2009), A learning community approach to doctoral education in the social sciences. *Teaching in Higher Education*, 14, no. 1, 43–54.

Pearson, M. and Brew, A. (2002), Research training and supervision development. *Studies in Higher Education*, 27, no. 2, 138–43.

Phillips, E. and Pugh, D. (2000), *How to get a PhD*, Buckingham: Open University Press (first edition published in 1987, third edition appearing in 2000).

Pilbeam, C. and Denyer, D. (2009), Lone scholar or community member? The role of student networks in doctoral education. *Studies in Higher Education*, 34, no. 3, 301–18.

Price, M., Handley, K., Millar, J. and O'Donovan, B. (2010), 'Feedback: All that effort, but What is the effect?' *Assessment and Evaluation in Higher Education*, 35, no. 3, 277–89.

Rose, M. (1980), Rigid rules, inflexible plans and the stifling of language: A cognitivist analysis of writers block. *College Composition and Communication*, 31, 389–401.

Somerville, E. and Crème, P. (2005), 'Asking Pompeii questions': A co-operative approach to Writing in the disciplines. *Teaching in Higher Education*, 10, no. 1, 17–28(12).

Scherer, K. R. (1984), On the nature and function of emotion: A component process approach. In K. R. Scherer and P. Ekman (eds), *Approaches to Emotion*, 293–317, Hillsdale, NJ: Erlbaum.

Stracke, E. and Kumar, V. (2010), Feedback and self-regulated learning: Insights from supervisors' and PhD examiners' reports. *Reflective Practice*, 11, no. 1, 19–32.

Thomson, P. and Kamler, B. (2016), *Detox your Writing*, London: Routledge.

Tinkler, P. and Jackson, C. (2004), *The Doctoral Examination Process: A Handbook for Students, Examiners and Supervisors*, London: Open University Press.

Trigwell, K. and Dunbar-Goddet, H. (2006), *The Research Experience of Postgraduate Research Students at the University of Oxford*, Oxford, Institute for the Advancement of University Learning. Available on-line at http://www.learning.ox.ac.uk/files/PGRreport.pdf

Vygotsky, L. (1962), *Thought and Language, Trans. Eugenia Hanfmann and Gertrude Vakar*, Cambridge, MA: MIT Press.

Weaver, M. (2006), Do students value feedback? Student perceptions of tutors' written responses. *Assessment & Evaluation in Higher Education*, 31, no. 3, 379–94.

Wellington, J. (2003), *Getting Published*, London: Routledge.

Wellington, J. (2013), Searching for Doctorateness. *Studies in Higher Education*, 38, no. 10, 1490–1503.

Wellington, J., Bathmaker, A., Hunt, C., McCulloch, G. and Sikes, P. (2005), *Succeeding with Your Doctorate*, London: Sage.

Wellington, J. and Sikes, P. (2006), 'A doctorate in a tight compartment': Why do students choose a professional doctorate and what impact does it have on their personal and professional lives. *Studies In Higher Education*, 31, no. 6, 723–34.

Wisker, G. (2001), *The Postgraduate Handbook*, London: Palgrave.

Woods, P. (1999), *Successful Writing for Qualitative Researchers*, London: Routledge.

INDEX

affective domain, *see* emotion
anxiety, anxiousness 48, 51, 59
assumptions 38
attitudes 47
audience 37, 45, 50–1
autonomy 132
avoidance, *see* denial

balance 66, 123–32, 109, 117, 123–4
barriers to being critical 98–9
beginnings 21–2
blocks 107–8
blogs 76
Bloom's Taxonomy 46
buddy 71–2
bullying 17
burnout 128–30

checkpoints 27
clarity 121
coaching 7-10, 107–17
comfort zone 65–6, 108–9
communities 4–7, 34, 68, 71, 74–7
community spirit 4–6
confidence 107, 112
confirmation report/review (CR) 24, 26–32
contribution 135–8

copyright 52
'criticality' 93–106
critical writing 103–4
crunch points 21–2
CR *viva* 28–30
cyclical process 26

deleting text 41–2
denial (ignoring, avoidance) 61, 108–9, 112–15
depression 130–2
development of writing 21, 22, 48–9, 60, 68, 76
'doctorateness' 132–8
doctorates 1–3, 134–8,143
drafting 40–1, 42, 122

effort 43
emotion 45–51
employability 146–50
epistemology 101–2
evaluating 101–3
examiners 138–41, 156,159
expectations 107–8, 110–11

fear 46, 48, 51, 59, 61, 115
feedback 27, 46, 63, 67–8, 113, 115, 117–22
feelings, *see* emotion
feeling stuck 107

first steps   34, *see also* 'getting
       started'
framing research   22

getting started   21–2, 32, 37, 59,
       63–4, 107, 113
'good' theses   141, 145–6

habit   32, 55–7, 60, 64
harassment   16
hidden work   70–1

individual   8, 60, 65, 72–4, 127
isolation   109–10, 115–17

Knowledge Telling
       model   59–60

literature base   25
literature reviews   79–91
live documents   26, 41, 64

mental health   126–32
mentoring   8–10, 55,
       71–4, 107
metacognition   100–1
metaphors for supervision   17–18
methodology   24–5, 29
milestones   21–2, 53–4
momentum   54, 56, 113
monitoring   54, 55, 61, 67
motivation   29, 37–8, 43–4

NHS Moodzone   131–2

ontology   101–2
oral examination   151–62
organization   39–40, 60
original contribution   29, 135–8
originality   135–8, 153
outcomes of confirmation
       review   31
outline   51–2

panic   129–30
peer support   33, 68, 71, 74–5,
       113–14, 116
perfect/perfection   68–9, 115
places for writing   42, 54–5,
       109, 116
planning   60–71, 111
postgraduate tutor   33, 122
post-thesis activity   162–5
post-*viva* activity   162–5
preparing for the *viva*   156–62
pressure, *see* stress
procrastination   66, 75, 112
product   9, 38, 62
project management   51–5
'Prompts'   62–3
proposal writing   22–6
publishing   162–3

readiness   38, 109, 113
reading   79–91
refining   25–6
reflexivity   99–100
relaxation, rest (breaks)   48, 53,
       75, 124–5
research proposal   22–6
research questions   24, 29
resilience   125–6
resource   51–2, 77
reviewers   27, 28
reviewing the literature   79–91
rewarding   50
risk   53
routine   32

schedule   40
searching the literature   82–8
self-care   123–32
self-coaching   7–10
Shut Up and Write   75
small and often   39–40, 55–7,
       62–3
social media   75–7, 117–18

stress   46, 48, 51, 127–8
submission (of thesis)   132–50
supervision   2–3, 10–19, 33–4, 52,
   68–70, 112, 115, 118–19
support services   34
support structures   6–7, 32, 34,
   117–19

theory, theoretical framework   23,
   25, 29
thesis mentoring   8–9, 55,
   71–3, 107
thinking   59, 113
time   13, 28, 32, 37–8, 40, 52–3,
   55–7, 66–7, 108, 119
time off, *see* relaxation

Transitions model   163–5
Twitter   76

upgrade, *see* confirmation review

viva behaviour   30, 161–2
viva questions   157–60
viva voce   26, 151–65

where to start   39
work in progress   114
worry, *see* anxiousness
writing about literature   86–91
writing groups   74–5
writing plans   57, 60–71,112
writing retreats   75–6